SECRET D

BOSSINEY BOOKS

First published in 1995
by Bossiney Books, St Teath, Bodmin, Cornwall.

Typeset and printed
by Penwell Ltd, Callington, Cornwall.

ISBN 1 899383 01 8

Front cover: Ray Bishop with model Eva Rutland
Drawings: Felicity Young

A DORSET church encapsulates the secret history of the past. ▶

About the Author

CLIVE GUNNELL is a West Country television presenter and director. His latest TV series, The Journeyman, recently seen on HTV and Channel Four, is a journey across South Western England including much of Dorset, and Clive has written a companion book to the series, also called **The Journeyman**, *published by Alan Sutton Books.*

Clive has lived and worked in the Westcountry for 40 years, filming the people and places he knows and loves.

Through his 'Walking Westward' series he became one of the best-known and best-loved figures in regional television. Though he and his wife Hilary live across the Dorset border in Somerset, he has a great affection for Dorset, having made many television programmes about the county. For HTVs 'Journeyman' Clive walked from Lulworth Cove along the coast to Lyme Regis. Here he makes a welcome reappearance as a Bossiney author setting the scene for **Secret Dorset**, *and recalling, among other things, the surprising fact that he once played cricket for a Dorset county team.*

SECRET DORSET

by Clive Gunnell

TELL me, do you want to know a secret? ran the words of a popular ballad of the fifties. And without exception the answer came back, oh yes please! Everybody has a secret of some kind and almost all are dying to share it with some other person or persons. When this secret concerns discovered places, romantic ruins, unknown locations of great scenic beauty, a village time has forgotten and the world bypassed, a virgin wood, or an untrodden sea-swept cliff-sheltered beach, then we can hardly wait to rush off and impart this discovery to anyone prepared to listen.

Upon returning to these idyllic locations afterwards and finding them, to our horror, choked with cars, their occupants, and our ears deafened by the mind-damaging noise of transistor radios, we become speechless with astonishment and indignation. How did so many people become aware of their existence? Who told them? Why can't they keep their mouths shut?

Nobody, absolutely nobody, has more awareness of this than myself. I have spent over thirty years seeking out such places all over the south west of England and then filming them for public perusal, entertainment, and approbation.

Today I am beginning to ask myself did I have the right to do this? Were not these places better left unknown and unvisited, and as a consequence unpolluted by the seemingly essential dirt, debris, and noise that has become a prerequisite of streams of visitors?

The only saving grace for my actions, and my satisfaction, lies in the enormous amount of letters I receive, telephone calls, and conversations in the street from the elderly, people in hospitals, and those who are no longer physically capable of travelling the routes I have taken, and as a consequence find their enjoyment journeying with me on film.

Some years ago I lived in a small cottage on the outskirts of Tavistock in Devon and spent all my free time walking Dartmoor. As a consequence I was asked to write about the moor for Bossiney Books. The book developed into a personal study of my life on Dartmoor, my friends and acquaintances, and a great many secret places, walks, views, and locations which I had by then come to consider my own private discoveries not to be disclosed or discussed with anyone. Many still remain secret to this day. Others I eventually turned into programmes for Westward Television, at that time the most regionally involved and integrated independent television company that ever existed, which, as a consequence lost its franchise for being, it was said, too parochial.

In this book, *My Dartmoor*, I revealed a number of secrets which included the whereabouts of what I had come to consider 'my tree'. It was on a walk from Kings Tor to Yelverton, leaving Royal Oak siding, part of the old Great Western Railway branch line that ran from Yelverton to Princetown and on its way crossed the tramway built in 1823 allowing granite to be taken from Swell Tor and Foggin Tor quarries and delivered to Plymouth in horse-drawn trucks. Not far from this tramway is a bridge that once carried the GWR steam engines and rolling stock from Princetown to Yelverton and on to Plymouth.

I remember sitting there surrounded by the debris of bygone industrial activity, in a mood of extreme sadness, haunted by those left-over dreams and ambitions, and the tragedy of wasted manpower, wasted mineral wealth, wasted opportunity, and the destruction of a magnificently beautiful railway line through the lush Devon countryside from Plymouth, on the splendour of Dartmoor from Roborough to Princetown. There is absolutely no doubt whatsoever in my mind that had this branch line been left intact and open it would today be one of the most successful and prosperous branch lines in existence, and very likely the most visited and used. And it was mulling these thoughts

TOLPUDDLE, famed for its martyrs and therefore holding a special place in not only Dorset but English history. According to the travel writer Arthur Mee, Tolpuddle took its name from the Danes who harried King Alfred, but, at heart, it is a very English place. This photograph, taken more than half a century ago, reflects a more leisurely tempo and way of Dorset life.

ANOTHER angle of Tolpuddle – this old photograph, probably taken in the 1930s, conveys the image of a quiet corner of the county. Yet dramatic events occurred here. One morning six farm labourers were called from their beds – arrested, they were taken to Dorchester to answer the serious charge of conspiracy. They earned just seven shillings a week, and they had joined a trade union in the hope of getting ten. But, as a warning to others, they were sent in chains to Australia for as long as seven years.

over in my mind, in a mood of deep depression brought on by my surroundings, that I suddenly spotted My Holly Tree.

Close by the bridge, sheltered by the bank as it sloped down to the tunnel entrance, it stood strong and proud, its trunk bent slightly as a concession to the prevailing wind, its foliage thick and olive green and its head shaved where the wind cleared the top of the embankment. Its presence there affected me like a trumpet blast of pure joy; triumphant and alone it was a symbol of challenge. Seeded by the wind or carried by a bird, it had flourished only where the blackthorn dared. Although Hucken Tor close by is lush with green, it is dwarf oak and mountain ash that cover those granite slopes down to the Walkham Valley, nor could you find another holly tree for miles around.

There is stood and stands still – for I visit it every year – defying the elements and making mockery of the cry that environment is the corner stone of survival. It has survived because it wanted to and not even the great blizzard of 1963 or the drought of 1976 has caused it to deviate from its purpose.

Through *My Dartmoor* I shared this secret with thousands, but none the less was astonished by the deluge of letters I received from people who sought out my tree and shared my joy. They had all set off across Dartmoor in search of the holly tree, and almost without exception had found this secret, and it had given them great pleasure by its presence.

So perhaps after all a secret shared in certain circumstances is not such a bad thing, and should be encouraged. Some secrets of course positively demand to be told and shared, particularly those concerning people of exceptional creative talent, and ability bordering upon genius, who are, nevertheless, neglected by those who ought to know better. These thoughts run through my mind as I sit in a tree-sheltered corner of my garden, where I come every evening at gin and tonic time, to catch the last warmth and splendour of the setting sun and gaze across the valley away to the Blackdown hills and beyond to the Dorset border. My view bypasses a magnificent American Oak tree, reputedly the third largest in Great Britain, although the way it is stretching and spreading it seems set to challenge the other two for that supremacy.

I have an overwhelming love for trees and am surrounded by them as I sit writing this, a great many of which I have planted, including the lilac tree grown from a root pulled out of the ground not more than eighteen inches high, that now, four years later, towers over my head, its resplendent blossoms brushing my neck, and its scent filling my nostrils with all the promise of May glory.

No one knew or understood this promise of May glory better than 'The Dorset Poet', William Barnes. He was born at Rush-Hay Farm, Bagber Common two miles west of Sturminster Newton, of farming stock, and his father supplemented his meagre earnings by hiring himself out to richer, more successful farmers.

Literary giant Thomas Hardy described him as: 'A lyric writer of high order of genius, probably the most interesting link between present and past forms of rural life that England possessed.'

H J Massingham declared: 'Peasant poetry miraculously reborn. All the sweetness and greenness of the Dorset pastures are in Barnes.'

And W H Auden proclaimed: 'I cannot enjoy one poem by Shelley, and yet am delighted by every line of William Barnes'.

None the less William Barnes remains, at least in my opinion, one of the genuine secrets of Dorset. He has quite rightly been referred to as: 'the greatest poet ever to have written in English dialect.'

Yet for every person who has read Thomas Hardy there are thousands who have never ever heard of William Barnes, and more than likely never will.

But who could better describe my lilac tree than this great poet, and in original Dorset language?

Dear lilac-tree, a-spreading wide
thy purple blooth on ev'ry zide
As if the hollow sky did shed
Its blue upon thy flow'ry head;
Oh! wether I mid sheare wi thee
Thy open air, my bloomen tree,
Or see thy blossoms vrom the gloom,
'Ithin my zunless worken-room,

My heart do leap, but leap wi'sighs,
At zight o' thee avore my eyes,
Vor when they grey-blue head do sway
In cloudless light, 'tis spring, 'tis May.

For a period after leaving Tavistock I lived in a tiny hamlet in Dorset not far from Evershot, and was about to spend a great deal of time discovering both William Barnes and Thomas Hardy country, and wallowing in the associations of fitting fact to fiction, and literary locations to the genuine articles. Naturally in the course of so doing I uncovered a great many Dorset secrets. It is almost impossible to move around Dorset in any direction without stumbling over some new and unknown, at least to one's self, connection with literature or art.

Travelling some time ago, from Mere just over the Dorset border in Wiltshire, after researching material concerning the school run for many years there by William Barnes, I was making my way back to my hotel in Shaftesbury and became hopelessly lost, in what many people who know me would classify as my usual manner. As always, I refused to ask for directions, believing I could sort things out for myself, and as a consequence failed miserably, but with surprisingly pleasant and informative results. I was travelling vaguely in the direction of Sturminster Newton and stopped at East Stour, and following a chance meeting with the local vicar I learned the farm I could see across the valley was once lived in by the celebrated novelist and playwright Henry Fielding, creator among many brilliant works, of *Tom Jones.*

He married a very beautiful lady from Salisbury, Charlotte Craddock, who had, for those times, a considerable bank balance. Fielding very quickly began to make inroads into this fortune – gaining a reputation for roistering and gambling in East and West Stour, Stalbridge, Sturminster Newton and wider afield – until the lady's money was all gone.

WILLIAM Barnes lives on in the shape of this statue in Dorchester. He lives on too in his verses – many good judges rate William Barnes the finest poet to have written in English dialect. His life and work underline the creative chemistry of Dorset – a very secret process. ▶

WILLIAM BARNES

Forced to return to London, he resumed work on his craft for the remainder of his life, but without ever recovering the financial resources and wellbeing he enjoyed whilst living in Dorset. His wife remained with him and upon her death Fielding almost immediately married her maid.

Nevertheless the memory of Charlotte Craddock will live for ever in the character of Sophia Weston in Fielding's finest work *Tom Jones*.

Within the following pages you will discover a delightful chapter by Michael Williams in which he has included a fascinating descriptive passage concerning, if he will pardon my saying so, one of his obsessional loves, cricket, in which he describes one of the most beautiful grounds in all England – in Dorset, naturally, at Cranford. It has always been a great mystery to me why the three most beautiful rural counties of England are not incorporated into the major county cricket league. Surely it cannot be because of lack of desire by visiting cricket teams and their spectators to visit these counties – after all their cars and caravans block the roads leading to the coasts of all three throughout the summer months. If they can travel and survive the surrounding architectural brutality of a visit to Old Trafford or the Oval, then visiting a county ground in Cornwall, Devon, or Dorset, would surely seem like the next best thing to a day trip to heaven. Certainly it is not lack of cricket interest in these three counties, for I have never known such enthusiastic response to the game, in hamlet, village, and town across the south west, and almost every ground a rural delight and joy.

Some of my happiest moments have been spent on the boundaries of these grounds fielding, exchanging anecdotes with the spectators, whilst occasionally imbibing a glass of the amber liquid, and watching my own side's bowlers belted all over the field. Westward Television had one of the most enthusiastic charity cricket sides for many years, and we travelled all over the Westcountry playing games to raise money for ground improvements, local charities, hospitals, and even church restoration funds.

Looking back I would find it impossible to choose the ground which I thought the most beautiful, or which had the finest surrounding aspect. I can easily recall the splendour of Paul Cricket Club in Cornwall, standing in the outfield looking down on the harbours of Mousehole and Newlyn, and away to West Penwith, St Ives and Land's End. Then there was the North Devon hilltop ground of Chumleigh, with the sunlight bouncing off the gorse and heather, creating grey blue shadows in the valleys and coombes of Exmoor in the far distance, where my attention was continually distracted by the belief I had seen a stag and deer.

But Dorset indeed boasts as fine as any, and Cattistock, the Dorset village side which Westward visited almost every year in the enveloping meadow and wooded surroundings of their ground, remains a special favourite. And one year having moved to Dorset to live in the next village I surprised the TV side by turning out for the local club to play against them.

There are so many more Dorset cricketing memories, including playing once for a Dorset County side against the Bishop's eleven at Sherborne to raise money for restoration to the Abbey, at the invitation of Mike Davis, one-time captain of Torquay and England rugby sides and then a master at Sherborne school.

This Sunday I walked out on to the gentle green slope that glides discreetly down to the Yeo, surrounded by woods and the glowing splendour of Sherborne's architecture, its magnificent Abbey built on the site of the ancient church of St Aldhem, during whose life, around 705, Sherborne school was built. Now 1,200 years after, the school still flourishes today as a seat of learning. Sherborne boasts two castles – one a ruin, the other in better condition, once owned by Sir Walter Raleigh sometime during 1594 – and street after street of delightful period architecture, including the Almshouses with cloister and chapel dating back to 1437.

On that day no cricket ground anywhere in the world could have given me half the pleasure or sense of occasion as did this ground, in the ancient capital of Newer Wessex, in the county of Dorset. Today if I wish to recall that time, all I need to do is take out the Dorset County tie I was presented with after the game, and memories flood back of the splendour and joy of this wonderful game of cricket. Something that William Barnes knew only too well.

Or at cricket, while one, in a quick handed flight
with the ball, saw in glory his wicket upright,
The ball fleetly roll'd and it sprang, and it flew,
It was out in the field, and at home at the shoe
Or it hit a man out,
Oh! he could not tell how;
While others would shout there
Well where are you now?

I have always had a great fondness for Poole, the only Dorset town to be built entirely on the Great Heath as it comes down to meet the channel. This famous Great Heath stretches back from Poole almost to the outskirts of Dorchester along the coast. Moving inland it extends to Bere Regis, linking back to Winfrith and connects up with the heath area of Purbeck. It was always a wide sweeping area of moorland, free of boundaries, unfenced, wild and uncultivated, and an army could have hidden there unseen and unknown.

Originally part of the Manor of Canford over six miles away, Poole obtained its first charter in 1248 from William de Longespee, son of Ela of Canford, and from that day forth the town developed and grew, from its humble beginnings as a small harbour on a waterside island, to the flourishing resort it has become today – its prosperity almost entirely due to the intensity of its sea trade. The Romans established a harbour here at Hamworthy, now incorporated into Poole. During its earliest days Poole was always being attacked from the sea, and its buildings razed to the ground, the townspeople fleeing to the sanctuary of the great heath and remaining there until the raiders had fled.

When Canute first started raiding Britain in 1015 it was at Poole that his marauding Danes landed and carried out their butchery and pillage. Its own maritime history is one of exceptional seamanship, and it is no Dorset secret to suggest its flourishing interest in piracy, and smuggling – particularly the kind of piracy so proudly encouraged by Elizabeth I and carried out so diligently by her favourite Admirals – contributed considerably to its increasing prosperity and trade. One of the undoubted master smugglers and pirates of all time was a Poole mariner Harry Page, who became the scourge of the English Channel, and a major thorn in the flesh of the French, who recognised him as 'Arripay'. At one stage in his career Arripay brought back to Poole 120 captured prize vessels taken off the coast of Normandy and Brittany. Spain also was not spared his ravages, whether stealing a most loved and revered crucifix from Cape Finisterre, or raising Gijon to the ground by fire. Finally despairing of any action being taken by the English authorities to curtail the activities of this most dedicated and successful pirate, the French and Spanish authorities – with the full approval and monetary support of the kings of Spain and France – fitted out a fleet for the sole purpose of attacking the Poole pirate in his den and destroying him.

This they most certainly did, and very successfully too. With great resolve and daring the combined fleets landed in Poole and a pitched battle was fought through the town. Even though Page was gallantly defended by the citizens of Poole, he was never the less forced to flee by the ferocity of the combined attackers, and like so many citizens of Poole before him, sought sanctuary and safety on the Great Heath.

It was no doubt because of the activities of Poole seamen on her behalf, that Queen Elizabeth I granted the town the right to become a county incorporate, and thus by the will of the Queen, Poole separated from the county of Dorset for a time.

In 1347 Poole willingly and with great speed, and at quite a high price of course, provided Edward III with four vessels and ninety-four men for the siege of Calais. Poole also bore witness to the ultimate and daring end of one of this nation's best kept secrets of all time – and unquestionably one of the greatest escape stories ever told – that of Charles II after the Battle of Worcester.

For weeks he had journeyed across England, from Worcester to Boscabel in the Midlands, here being forced to hide in the pouring rain concealed in the green foliage of an oak tree's boughs, whilst the Parliamentary cavalry, worn out with searching, rode past beneath, heads bent down trying to avoid the blinding rain – as every child who once wore an oak-apple cluster on oak-apple day knows well.

From there he moved westward to Bristol, and finally journeyed across threequarters of Dorset, first to the delightful village of Trent where he was hidden by his brave and most loyal travelling companion, Colonel Wyndham, in the manor house which was his family home. Charles occupied Lady Anne Wyndham's room which had access to a hiding place with a double floor under the roof. Here whilst trying to sleep one afternoon Charles was continuously disturbed by the non-stop ringing of the church bells. Upon enquiry he was informed the bells were being rung to celebrate the death of King Charles II.

Trent is a most charming village and the manor house stands as proud and handsome today as it must have looked when Charles was in residence. The village church is also a very pleasant building and worth a visit to see the most interesting and masterly carved bench ends to be found anywhere.

Across from the Manor House stands the village inn, the Rose and Crown, once owned and run by an old friend and colleague of mine, and I have enjoyed many good evenings in its bar, even on occasions serving behind it, in convivial and jovial company. Col Wyndham is buried in the churchyard, as is his wife who took such enormous risks in hiding the King, often alone, as her husband would be out finding a safe route to convey the King to the coast.

This they finally achieved, first to Charmouth, seeking a boat to carry them over to France. Whilst there one of the party required a blacksmith to attend to a shoe on his horse. The King moved on to Bridport where he rested at the George Inn, no longer there today. The last time I visited, it had become an antique shop. Charles was masquerading as a manservant to Col Wyndham, and here he waited for the others to arrive from Charmouth. When they did arrive it was bearing the news that the very observant blacksmith had noticed the horses' shoes were shod in what was known in the trade as the Worcester fashion. His suspicions were aroused, and he reported the possible presence of the King in the area to the Roundhead officer.

Whilst the Parliamentary troops were assembling for the chase, the King's party had to await the arrival of Lord Wilmot, and then immediately fled the town in the direction of Dorchester on the High Road, but they very quickly turned off along a narrow byway today known as Lee Lane. Here an engraved stone still marks his route.

King Charles II
Escaped capture through this lane.
September XXIIL. MDCLI.

The most fascinating thing concerning this whole adventure for me is that as far as anyone knows, throughout the entire route of Charles' escape, this one incident in Charmouth was the only occasion in which a citizen reported the possible presence of the King.

How this man kept the secret of his whereabouts hidden away from the people of the areas through which he passed I cannot understand. By all accounts Charles stood well over six feet tall, at a time when five foot ten would have been above average height. He had a swarthy Mediterranean complexion, a large slightly hooked nose, with luxuriant dark hair in waves – at least so reads one of the many proclamations announcing his escape and requesting information for his capture. It also placed a reward on his head equivalent to almost a million pounds in today's money, and yet no one informed against him – not even the people who had suffered hurt or disgrace under his father, although a great many of them must have had some knowledge of his whereabouts and intent. Moreover one of the party travelling with the king in his escape had a great fondness for alcohol and an uncontrollable tongue. Yet apart from this once chance recognition his escape and intent remained a secret.

Charles' route from Lee Lane eventually led him by evening to the Dorset village of Broadwindsor, where his party halted and acquired rooms for the night of September 23. They stayed in the 'Castle', burnt down in 1856 and no longer a hostelry today. Broadwindsor was at one time renowned for the number of sheep which flourished on the slopes of the surrounding hills, and also for the growing of flax destined for the nearby village of Slape, where there was once a mill. During the night in the inn the king's party was awakened by the arrival of the Roundhead cavalry demanding beds and ordering that the occupants be put out of their rooms at once. Fortunately one of their travelling ladies decided it was a good time to give birth and during the confusion the royal party slipped away and returned to Trent to work out their next move.

This final move took the party to Mere in Wiltshire, from there to Hele House not far from Salisbury, awaiting the last stage of the escape, which brings us back to Poole.

On the evening of October 16 1651, a small coal brig named Surprise sailed into Poole haven and dropped anchor. This was not at all unusual as this vessel plied between Poole and Shoreham regularly with its cargo of coal, and the fact that she was a day late could have easily been explained by the loss of wind or tide.

But when the skipper, by name of Tatersall, stepped ashore he had a wonderful tale to tell that had nothing to do with carrying coal. No! His cargo had been far more precious, far more important, and its loss could have changed the whole course of British history.

Yes, he said, he had as usual left Shoreham on the morning of the previous day – but not to return to Poole. Oh no! He had crossed the channel to France to Fecamp, and his journey had netted him sixty pounds, and, no, he was not telling them lies.

What kind of cargo had he aboard that was worth that amount of money? his listeners enquired.

Two gentlemen who urgently wanted to go to France, Tatersall replied.

And what manner of gentlemen would pay such an enormous amount of money for a passage to France?

Why, His Majesty King Charles and my Lord Wilmot, forsooth, flying the country after the battle of Worcester.

After the Restoration, Charles ordered the brig Surprise be brought to London and moored on the Thames by Whitehall where he could see it. He further ordered her name be changed to the Royal Escape, and awarded Tatersall a one-hundred pound pension, also allowing him to remain her master with a salary, as the vessel was now entered into the Navy as a 'fifth-rate'. And there the brig remained until 1791 when, completely rotten and waterlogged, she was broken up and burned.

I have journeyed every inch of the route taken by Charles II during his escape, and visited most of the houses and buildings that gave him shelter along the way, particularly across Dorset, and it is my fondest wish to make a dramatised documentary film one day of this epic escape.

Poole harbour holds a particularly fond place in my heart, and remembrance of a truly magnificent Westcountry achievement.

Some years ago the tiny shipbuilding yard of Alan Hinks, on the Taw Torridge estuary in Appledore, North Devon, won a commission to build a perfect replica of a sixteenth century ketch, the Nonsuch. This vessel was to be built exactly as she would have been during the 16th century, as far as possible to be hand-built and of no modern materials but all wood, including the fastenings and fittings.

She was commissioned by the Hudsons Bay Company in England to present to the Hudsons Bay Company of Canada, to mark the anniversary of the discovery of Hudsons Bay by this vessel. The ship on arrival was to be set in concrete as near to the spot where she was originally moored as was possible. Despite this eventual future she had however to be a perfect sailing boat in every way, and it was intended to sail her around the west coast of England, stopping at most of the sea ports along the way, to allow people to come aboard. It was also intended to sail her along the east coast of Canada before securing her in her final resting place.

Hearing of this project I wrote to the Hudsons Bay Company asking if I could make a film of the entire project from the laying of the keel upwards. To my utter amazement they said yes, and I was told to go ahead at once.

We filmed every month of her progress up to the moment of her launching. This became a glorious local event, the banks of the estuary surrounding the boatyard and the sand beaches of Braunton lined with holiday makers in festive mood, the water crowded with every conceivable kind of private, pleasure, and working boat. Overhead hovered helicopters from RAF Chivenor with search lights rotating and distress and signal rockets cracking and thundering into sunbursts as the Nonsuch came down the ramp – and I was aboard.

Her masts were fitted at Appledore Shipbuilders, at that time the finest, most revolutionary, and first completely covered shipbuilding yard in Europe, and today, like Alan Hinks yard, closed down and idle, due almost entirely to successive government disinterest and the greed of financial speculators. Then Nonsuch sailed from Appledore around Land's End, visiting ports and resorts throughout the south west, taking visitors aboard and in every way demonstrating the artistry and craftsmanship of Westcountry shipbuilders.

Eventually she arrived under full canvas in Poole harbour, and I was still aboard.

The skipper of Nonsuch, Captain Adrian Small from Brixham – who had sailed in every capacity on almost every vessel under canvas, from deckhand to master, including passages around Cape Horn – told me he had to return home and remain several days, and invited me to have full use of the captain's cabin whilst he was away. This I speedily complied with, and as a result twenty four hours later I was to experience the most moving, the most exciting and revealing episode of my life, and one with such limitless possibilities and opportunities for the future of mankind it was almost impossible fully to comprehend.

Adrian's cabin was entirely 16th-century, he had somehow managed to keep every necessity of modern existence, every artefact, every mechanical and electrical device essential for modern shipping safety, somehow hidden away out of sight, or placed just outside the cabin in easy handling distance for an emergency. I was in a genuine 16th-century cabin, and stood there looking at the same fixtures and fittings, sleeping accommodation, captain's table, as did the original skipper of the Nonsuch over four hundred years ago. Nothing broke the illusion of my being in a bygone age, even the radio speaker had been concealed in a cupboard.

I finally retired to bed, and awoke very early in the morning as dawn was breaking to gaze out of my porthole at the emerging architectural splendour of Poole waterfront. I lay in my bunk, feeling Nonsuch gently moving on her mooring with the wind and tide, listening to the radio. Quite suddenly to my utter amazement I realised I was listening to two men landing on the moon. There I lay encased in a craftsman-constructed cocoon of past history, built for the sole purpose of seeking out new lands, unexplored waters, and to open up undiscovered areas of this world, in search of breathing space and the fresh, exciting, rewarding, opportunities that would follow. And I lay listening to the beginning of the future of the new world – a world where the modern generations of adventurers must go to seek their inheritance, where the true descendants of Drake, Hawkins, Frobisher and Raleigh, I feel, must go in order to perpetuate the continuation of the human race. Out there is infinite, its possibilities immense, unimaginable, in size and scope, and it is imperative the coming generations go there in order to advance and continue human existence and knowledge.

This I firmly believe. These unstoppable thoughts went racing around my brain aboard Nonsuch, and I will cherish the memory of that morning in Poole harbour as long as I live.

During the period I lived in Dorset, it was my delight every Saturday morning to leave my home and head off in the direction of the coast, with the intention of undertaking my weekly shopping, but quite naturally not intending to let this essential act interfere too drastically with such other pursuits, pleasures or persuasions that might intervene along the way. Firstly, as it was always early when I set off, I would require breakfast and for this I went to the tiny harbour of West Bay.

Here on its pebble stone beach stood a cafe – not renowned for its architectural splendour, but certainly for its breakfasts – and as far as I could ascertain it never seemed to close. Whatever time I arrived it always seemed to have customers, many already served and busy putting away enormous fried breakfasts.

Mostly they were fishermen, some just back from lifting their crab and lobster pots and removing the catch, having left long before dawn light, now ready to land their catch, and most probably, as in fishing ports all over the Westcountry, spend Saturday morning having a 'make and mend' aboard, until retiring for a lunchtime pint or two.

Others were obviously just about to leave for sea, either for the same reason, to empty their pots, or they were taking out parties of anglers who had hired their boats for the day, a very popular pursuit in the summer months. There might also be a few dedicated walkers along the Dorset Coast Path, from east or west cliffs – neither terribly hard climbs, at least in comparison with Golden Cap which those proceeding westward would be conquering in their next few miles. Eastward is not so bad over the sandstone cliff alongside the Golf Course, where the coast path encroaches nearer and nearer to the playing area, and at times on to it, as the cliff erosion continues

unabated.

It is a miracle that these magnificent cliffs exist at all. And most certainly they would not today were it not for the existence of the Chesil Bank, believed thrown up in one night's gale. This incredible length of pebble ridge stretches in a stately curve eighteen miles from Portland to West Bay and has pebbles which for some unaccountable reason diminish in size from quite large stones in the more sheltered beach off Portland to tiny pebbles by the time they reach West Bay. Without its protection almost everything lying behind it would have been washed away years ago, along with the harbour of West Bay, and my breakfast.

Everything about West Bay fascinates me, even the fact that it is the port of Bridport. Why Bridport decided it required the worry and expense of a port I have no idea, but I am overjoyed that it did because I like coming here, and of course today it has the added responsibility of being an integrated and most vital part of coast protection. Time and time again the two piers jutting out into the channel that form the harbour entrance have been washed away and destroyed by wind and tide, and equally as often replaced. Today of course that replacement is compulsory, as it is with the celebrated cobb at Lyme Regis.

Certainly there cannot be a more difficult harbour to enter or leave than this one, with its long narrow opening between two piers, wide enough, just, to take a typical Westcountry trawler or crabbing boat, but most certainly nothing larger, and of course anything above a moderate wind and the harbour is closed to all shipping. Nevertheless it seems to provide a living for a number of working fishing boats, none better than the crabbing boat of Dave Sale, whom I featured in my Channel Four series the Journeyman and wrote about in *The Journeyman* book. I can vouch for the fact that his fish go straight to his restaurant, created from a restored barn on the outskirts of Bridport towards Dorchester, by the turning off to the Golf Club. Here his wife supervises some of the most delicious fish food I have ever eaten. West Bay, for such a small

◀ *OLD buildings and ruins fire our speculation and curiosity. Here is an artist's impression of how Corfe Castle may have looked in 1643.*

place, is unique in that it can boast two such unexcelled fish restaurants, for its famous Riverside near the harbour, which started life as a fish and chip restaurant, the finest I have eaten anywhere, and still providing this service, has over the years become recognised as one of the finest fish restaurants in the country.

For the walker on the Coast Path there can be no more challenging yet purposeful adventure than leaving West Bay, climbing West Cliff upwards and onwards towards the gloriously rewarding heights of Golden Cap. From this vantage point the view is unsurpassed in beauty and grandeur anywhere in the world. Inland, the undulating Dorset countryside is an unbroken square carpet of green meadow, golden wheat, ploughed brown earth, with darker less regulated patches of deep green conifer, contrasting against the lighter greens of broadleaf wood and copse – the whole illustrating the unmatched splendour of Marshwood Vale. Seaward there is a coastline often on a clear day visible to Start Point, and back following the curved cliffs to Portland. It's a wondrous place, particularly at sunrise when, clearing the horizon, the sun's first rays like scarlet pokers illuminate the tops of the sandstone cliffs into burnished gold, and beneath, the sea mist lingering on sea and land like a blue-grey gauze, allows the summit of Golden Cap to float unsupported in the upper air, breathless and still. No birds fly, not a sound breaks the dreamlike quality, the unreality of its Arabian Nights magic, until suddenly the croaking scream of a nesting seagull explodes the silence bringing the walker back to earth, and settling Golden Cap back on its foundations again. This is the Golden Cap I will always take with me in my memory, to draw on again and again, to sustain me when times become difficult.

Before leaving West Bay I always take a walk around the harbour area, with its three pubs, and visit the site of what used to be its ship building yard in Victorian days, and good boats they were too. I have a reason for this, dating back to the days when I lived in Brixham, and for a short time owned and worked a small clinker-built crabbing boat from West Bay, with a tiny cabin on the stern no bigger and exactly shaped like a telephone box. I could steer with my arm and hand sticking out of the back. There are still a number of these in West Bay harbour today. On my way back to my cottage in order to undertake the main reason for my journey, I always made for Beaminster.

There was an excellent reason for this, it was to easy to shop in this town, its car park being situated in the centre, on what was so obviously the town square. So having parked it was a simple matter to walk from shop to shop around the square carrying one's purchases, visiting butcher, baker, greengrocer, etc without having to keep crossing the road, and no distance from the car. But then I like Beaminster, particularly because of its lasting connection with Thomas Hardy, principally through Tess of the D'Urbervilles, where Beaminster became Hardy's, Emminster. I like it also because of my deep and abiding friendship with the best researcher I have ever worked with, David Middlemiss. He is not a Dorset man but his love, understanding, and knowledge of Dorset, and in particular those connected with Thomas Hardy are monumental. He has lived here for the greater part of his life and has been invaluable to my own knowledge and appreciation of this county for years. He has also been instrumental in acquiring, and producing the facts and information on almost all the films I have made in Dorset over the past twenty-five years, including The Journeyman and in particular 'A Winter Journey'.

It was during the making of this film we uncovered what was surely the best kept Dorset secret for years.

'A Winter Journey' told the story, using Hardy's poetry and prose, of the walk made by Tess of the D'Urbervilles from Flintcombe Ash farm where she had gone to work in the dairy, fifteen miles across the Dorset countryside, to the town of Emminster. We followed every foot of this fictional walk, David having spent months fitting Hardy's names and locations and descriptive passages to the actual scenes and places as they are today, and it was astonishing to find almost every location had remained almost untouched, unspoilt, and mostly unaltered. It was a revelation – leaving the farm climbing the escarpment, looking down on the Vale of Blackmoor, climbing Dogberry Hill and High Stoy towards the Devil's Kitchen and arriving eventually at Cross in Hand.

Cross in Hand is as desolate a spot today as it must have been when the stone column called the cross was first erected in the hedge at the side of the road. It stands on Batcombe Down surrounded by miles of open heath and the occasional ploughed field, hardly a tree protects the traveller from the almost incessant wind and rain. Here it was that Tess swore an oath to Alec D'Urberville that she would tempt him no longer, and she swore it on the cross, believing it to be a cross that could, and had, worked miracles. Later however as she continued home she met an old man and asked him about the cross, and he replied, it was a cross of evil where a wrongdoer was brought and nailed to it through his hands and left there.

To be honest nobody seems to know why the four-foot high stone column was erected or when, although all manner of elaborate claims surround it. Some are convinced there was once a hand carved on the stone to hold a metal bowl into which passers-by placed money for the poor, others insist there was a large cross at the top of the column which has been broken off and disappeared, it was put there to lighten the footsteps of Christian wayfarers. Its most probable use was as a boundary marker stone, for parish, county or even farmland.

Certainly no more isolated or deserted a spot could have been chosen for such a road marker.

Not far along the road lies the almost deserted village of Batcombe, at the foot of a terrifying drop in the road, down a winding ever-falling lane, bordered by green foliage of hedgerow and wood, leading to the location of the village church, surrounded on three sides by the almost straight up sides of the Downs. The church tower is quite famous, not because of the splendour of its architecture, but because of the pinnacles that stand at each corner, four in all, although the tower's fame dates from the time when there were only three. The fourth, it would seem, had been knocked down by an astonishing feat of horsemanship by the one-time squire of the village, John Minterne, better known as Conjuring Minterne, because of his relationship with the Devil, which it was believed he used to keep the villagers in awe and fear of him. This most famous feat performed by the squire was to jump his horse, it is alleged, from the edge of the downs above the church, down to the village, over the top of the church tower. Unfortunately on his way down one of the horse's hooves kicked off one of the tower pinnacles, and the tower remained in this state for many years. The church has memorial tablets and a grave stone to John Minterne, but they do not seem to be commemorating Minterne. The most likely grave is the one that does not seem to know whether it is in or outside the church, and this makes a great deal of sense, for Conjuring Minterne always insisted he would be buried neither in nor outside the village church, and it would seem his wish was granted. However there does seem to be one serious omission. Despite searching endlessly I could find no memorial of any kind commemorating the remarkable feat executed by the horse, which I most certainly believe deserves recognition of some kind, and a word or two concerning its bloodstock line might assist a great many punters on Grand National day.

For Tess, her journey ended in the town of Beaminster, Thomas Hardy's Emminster. Here she hoped to meet her father-in-law, the Reverend Clare, to ask news of her husband Angel Clare, who had left her and fled to South America. Sadly she never accomplished this, and her life from that moment was doomed to its eventual end on the gallows.

During the making of this film, I was fortunate, through the actions of David Middlemiss to be introduced, in her home in Beaminster, to an elderly lady, Gertrude Bugler, who, as a young girl had been chosen to play the part of Tess, in the Dorchester Amateur Dramatic Society's first-ever production of this play, adapted by Thomas Hardy especially for them.

The opening night was attended by Thomas Hardy, who was accompanied by a great many distinguished theatrical personalities, including producers, and impresarios, and as a direct result the play was commissioned to be put on in the West End at the Duke of York theatre. However Thomas Hardy absolutely insisted that Gertrude Bugler be given the role of Tess, which she was. She allowed me to interview her on film, and she described how she felt being in London for the first time, how she enjoyed playing the role, and being interviewed by theatre critics, who she said, always wanted to know the same thing, why did Thomas Hardy pick you? She described the fun of being wined and dined and generally entertained by the dashing young blades of her day, and meeting famous people, not only from the world of theatre, but many others, painters, writers, and celebrities of every kind. When the run ended she was offered other parts of many kinds, but to everyone's amazement declined all offers, returned to Dorset and picked up her life exactly as it was before going to London. That is how she continued, to the day I talked to her, with no regrets of any kind.

We had stopped filming, allowing her to relax, get her breath back, and perhaps remember other interesting occasions in her life she had perhaps not mentioned, when quite suddenly, with not a camera rolling, and no sound recording, she said: 'Young man' – I was in my late fifties at the time – 'Young man, you are the only one of all the people who have come to talk to me about my life with Thomas Hardy, and my performing in Tess, you are the only one who has not said, what did Thomas Hardy give you? What did you get from Thomas Hardy? What did he give you?

'Well I'll tell you. The only thing I ever got from Thomas Hardy was the same thing he gave everybody else.

'A very limp handshake!'

Gertrude Bugler died shortly after this interview, but I have always believed, that afternoon, without asking for it, I came into the possession of the best-kept Dorset secret of all time.

In front of me whilst I have been writing is a document from a national organisation, that has a comprehensive and passionate involvement with all things environmental in the country. It informs me that between 1995 and the year 2006 it is intended to build 100,000 houses in the county of Devon, and almost before the date on this document had dried, the Government source from whence it came had added the additional sum of a further 68,000 houses, which had been underestimated in their previous assessment. There is of course no estimate of the new roads, industrial estates, schools, hospitals, and ever larger supermarkets that will need to be built to cater for all this development in the rural areas.

I write this because I passionately believe that some time in the future an enlightened government, in order to ensure that future generations will have some idea what a truly rural county looked like, and how breathtakingly beautiful it could be, will pass a law insisting that a certain number of counties throughout Great Britain, from that moment on will remain exactly as they are for the rest of time. No one will be allowed in unless the same number of persons leave. No more building, no new roads scarring the landscape, no more electric pylons marching in all their technological arrogance across the skyline, as they do across the splendour of Marshwood Vale. In effect a living example of all that was best of past generations and the landscape in which they lived throughout history. A dream, of course, but other people without power have 'had a dream' and watched it come to fruition.

If my dream should ever come to pass, then the first English county chosen has to be Dorset. Nowhere, absolutely nowhere I know, has retained the feel, the aspect, the dignity of life, and lives, as much as this county, whilst at the same time preserving its landscape and seascape almost in its original condition. There have been changes obviously, but not of such magnitude or contempt for the past that has occurred almost everywhere else.

Dorset has managed somehow to retain the greatest of all its gifts, its unsullied, and undefeated poetical ambience. Just how this has been accomplished is unquestionably Dorset's greatest secret of all – and long may it be preserved.

About the Author

MICHAEL WILLIAMS, a Cornishman, started full-time publishing in 1975. He and his wife Sonia live in a cottage on the shoulder of a green valley just outside St Teath in North Cornwall.

His recent publications include **Psychic Phenomena of the West** *and his highly acclaimed* **Supernatural Search in Cornwall** *has been reprinted.*

Outside his Bossiney activities, Michael Williams is a writing and publishing consultant, evaluating manuscripts and advising writers on their publishing prospects.

In addition to publishing and writing, Michael Williams is a keen cricketer and collector of cricket books and autographs. He was the first captain of the Cornish Crusaders Cricket Club and is today President of the Crusaders. He is also a member of Cornwall and Gloucestershire County Cricket Clubs – and a Vice-President of the Cornwall Rugby Football Union. A member of the International League for the Protection of Horses and the RSPCA, he has worked hard for reform in laws relating to animal welfare.

He makes regular visits to Dorset on book business, and rates it one of his favourite counties in all England. Here he looks at the creative spirit of Dorset and provides a Cornish perspective. Bossiney publishing covers an area from Bournemouth across to Bristol and all the way down to Cornwall.

A CORNISH PERSPECTIVE of Secret Dorset

by Michael Williams

CREATIVITY is a secret process and here in the most English of counties a great deal has been achieved in book form and art. The question and the answer remain elusive. Maybe it is something to do with the secrets of Dorset and the eternal quest of men and women for the unknown.

The eminent Cornish painter Margo Maeckelberge once said to me: 'The most important thing to me is this mysterious X, an artist must *feel* about a place to paint it ...'

Perhaps that is why creative spirits are drawn to Dorset. It cannot be an accident or a coincidence.

The wonderful diversity of the terrain may have something to do with it too: the underlying rock, the limestone and the chalk, the sand and the clay. We climb a hill or round a corner, and suddenly we find ourselves in *another* Dorset. There are so many Dorset images. The arable fields, those tree lined pastures, that desolate unproductive heath, rocky bays and beautiful beaches: Dorset in its highly individual way personifies the best of England – though we will find no mountains or brooding moors.

You may think I am exaggerating the variety, but take a look at the coastline alone and you will get your answer. This Dorset coast is incredible in its contrast and often breathtaking in its beauty, switching from the gentle character of Poole Harbour to the sheer savagery of the cliffs at Purbeck and the majesty of the seaboard beyond Bridport.

There is an enigmatic something in the fabric of Dorset history: the wreckings of Chesil Beach, the robberies of Cranborne Chase, the sadism of the Bloody Assize, but you cannot think of Judge

Jeffreys as you eat your cream tea on a sunlit afternoon – at least I cannot – and herein lies Dorset's strength. The county's face may be distorted for a while – but only for a while.

Paul Nash, that distinguished English painter of landscape and still life, more than half a century ago reflected: 'On a sunny day the delightful vagaries of the Chase are enchanting to watch under the changing lights. The Bank, lapped by a blue sea, fringed by tamarisk, and harbouring a thousand swans, is only a pleasant dream, as you lie on Abbotsbury Hill.'

The creative forces at work in Dorset are a two-way process. Creative characters have been drawn – and continue to be drawn to the county life magnets – and these men and women have brought with them considerable gifts and, in return, Dorset has given them something too. Furthermore I predict the pattern will continue. Others will come in the future, drawn by some magnetism and, provided they have vision and respond, then new masterpieces will be shaped in words or paint, pottery or sculpture.

Nobody personified the creative spirit of Dorset more vividly than the sculptor Elisabeth Frink. I find it difficult to write of her in the past tense; she died in 1993 but lives on in her sculptures housed in churches and galleries and public places throughout Great Britain and other parts of the globe.

The most celebrated British sculptor of her generation, Elisabeth Frink lived at Woolland, shaping her characters in her studio or working out of doors. Her final major commission, *Risen Lord*, was finished and positioned in Liverpool's Anglican Cathedral – the England cricketer David Sheppard's cathedral – shortly before her death. You will find one of her rare female figures closer to home. Her bronze Walking Madonna, sculpted in 1981, stands in the gracious Close of Salisbury Cathedral.

As an animal lover I have a special affection for her horses and dogs. Her *Horse* for Goodwood is a noble creature. It was commissioned by the Earl of March. Interestingly, the sculptor maintained it was not meant to be an exact replica of a thoroughbred but her *idea* of a racehorse. Her horses are more to do with the ancient equine spirit which has played such a role in history and culture.

In the summer of 1994 Sonia's grand-daughter Gemma was in hospital at Dorchester, and we visited her there one Sunday after-

THE creative spirit of Dorset at the turn of the century: Sherborne Pageant.

noon. All three of us sat on the patio and talked. We were not alone. A beautiful Frink dog stood beside us and, as in Barbara Hepworth's garden in St Ives more than thirty years ago, I felt in the presence of something or someone very special. In that Cornish garden all those calendars ago Barbara Hepworth walked around it with me, and curiously on that recent Sunday in Dorchester I sensed Elisabeth Frink was not far away.

I confessed to Dame Barbara I did not understand some of her work – the fault was mine not hers – and she said: 'I'll leave you for a quarter of an hour … just wander round and let them speak to you.' Thirty years on, and a little wiser, Elisabeth Frink's dog spoke to me. Elisabeth Frink once said something to the effect that she liked the idea of people strolling by and thinking 'There's something over there … watching us.' Not only two great sculptors but kindred spirits. When the two met there must have been a kind of electricity.

Yes, a creative chemistry here in Dorset and Elisabeth Frink responded to it with great energy and imagination, and when we meet her work we feel a splendid sense of occasion.

I first became aware of Dorset's creativity as a young Cornishman years before I ever crossed the border dividing it from Devon. Back in 1957 Dr Charles Causley put together a marvellous anthology of verse from the Westcountry. Published by Macdonald of London, it contained an evocative poem *The Haunting* by Laurence Whistler of Lyme Regis and a short poem *At Max Gate* by Siegfried Sassoon with reference to 'Hardy, the Wessex wizard.' Even then I knew Dorset must be a rather special place.

You cannot write about the creativity of Dorset and fail to mention Thomas Hardy.

Down to the last days of his early life, when he was generally regarded as the greatest living Englishman, Hardy retained an unconscious simplicity. One magazine editor recalled how Hardy sent in his poems timidly, rather like a beginner, almost apologising and offering to correct any mistakes.

G K Chesterton said: 'Hardy has not only given us the air of the Westcountry; it is but just to say that he has given us the earth, the common clay, the stones and certainly the thorns and weeds.'

I am writing this chapter at a desk in North Cornwall, a corner of Cornwall which has strong Hardy links. It was to St Juliot in 1872 that Hardy, then a young architect, came to assist in the restoration of the church. He arrived at the Rectory on a Monday evening in march, a recently written poem sticking out of a pocket. A fateful evening it proved, for he was received by Emma Lavina Gifford, sister-in-law of the Rev Caddell Holder, the incumbent, a woman of 29 with corn-coloured hair who, four years later, became the first Mrs Hardy. Though no beauty, Emma Gifford could be vivacious. She had a good figure, rode well and was genuinely interested in literature.

In a manuscript discovered after her death, she recalled their romance: 'My architect came two or three times a year ... I rode my pretty mare Fanny, and he walked by my side, and I showed him more of the neighbourhood – the cliffs along the roads, and through the scattered hamlets, sometimes gazing down at the solemn small shores below, where seals lived, coming out of the great deep caverns occasionally ... often we walked to Boscastle

THOMAS Hardy who personified and continues to personify Dorset to a remarkable degree in the minds of his readers.

Harbour down the beautiful Valency Valley where we would jump over a low wall by rough steps or get through a narrow pathway to come out on great wide spaces suddenly, with a little brook, going the same way, in which we once lost a tiny picnic tumbler, and there it is to this day no doubt between two of the boulders.' An incident which Hardy used in his poem *Under the Waterfall.*

'Sometimes we drove to Tintagel and Trebarwith Strand, where donkeys were employed carrying seaweed to the farmers; Strangles beach, also Bossiney, Bude and other places along the coast. Lovely drives they were, with sea views all along at intervals ...'

Sadly the marriage turned sour and for more than thirty years they existed in disharmony. Yet after Emma's death, Hardy, looking back on those earlier romantic times, came back to Cornwall: a return which triggered some of his most moving work, probably some of the greatest love poems ever written.

Beeny Cliff, to the north of Boscastle, inspired what must be one of the most magical opening lines ever shaped by Cornwall's creative spirit: 'O the opal and the sapphire of that wandering open sea ...'

Boscastle, a lovely Cornish village at the edge of the sea, is, in fact, the Castle Boterel in Hardy's novel *A Pair of Blue Eyes*, the story of a young architect coming to Endelstow in North Cornwall in connection with a church restoration, a romance that ends with the lovers travelling on the same train, one a corpse inside a coffin.

A Cornish perspective? 'I wonder how many know of Jack Clemo's fruitful relationship with Dorset and Weymouth in particular.

Jack Clemo was one of our greatest native Cornish writers: a poet of power and rare religious insight, autobiographer, novelist and essayist. Deaf and blind, he lived for many years with his mother in the heart of the china clay country – Cornwall's lunar landscape – in a granite cottage within the shadow of the claypits. There was something of Blake and Bunyan in his make-up. He was quite simply one of the most original writers in Britain this century

Jack Clemo, despite enormous problems of deafness and blindness, held the belief that his destiny was to marry – and marry he did. His marriage to his wife Ruth in 1968 produced a transformation in his literary vision, and after his mother's death they came to live in Dorset, Ruth's native county.

I had visited him at his china clay country cottage, back in 1963, before Ruth had come onto the scene, and asked him about writers he admired and how he defined the poet – his mother read his correspondence and then painstakingly translated the contents by tracing each letter, each word onto the palm of his hand.

Here is the reply:

'The three great writers who most deeply influenced me are Browning, D H Lawrence and Hardy. Much of my early verse was modelled on Browning and it was from him that I derived my robust Christian optimism and my contempt for what he called "poetics" in the approach to romantic emotion. Lawrence influenced me chiefly as a sex mystic. He was both an affinity and a pagan challenge which I had to answer, while the lyrical beauty of his prose style gave me more aesthetic pleasure than that of any other writer. Hardy influenced me chiefly as an interpreter of landscape and through the immediacy of his portrayal of village life and character.

THOMAS Hardy's birthplace, Rockhampton.

'I believe the true poet is an interpreter and a priest detached as an artist from the obvious aspects of religious truth, but illuminating them from a unique angle of personal vision, not substituting for them a world of pure subjectivity. I dislike technical experiments which merely dazzle readers and sidetrack them from a working philosophy instead of helping them to understand the deeper meanings of life.'

It is interesting to reflect that Dorset, in the person of Thomas Hardy, touched him before Ruth came into his life. After their marriage in 1968 – Dr Charles Causley, the distinguished Cornish poet was his best man – Ruth assumed the role of his literary communicator, using the same painstaking letter to palm technique, and whatever Ruth told him went deep. When they enjoyed a summer's walk in a garden, her commentary triggered a fine poem.

In 1984 they came to live in her home town of Weymouth and his creativity flowed. His work became gentler – though no less perceptive – and visits to Italy increased the process.

In Weymouth Baptist Church he enjoyed Christian fellowship and the deep peace for which he had longed. His death in July 1994 marked the end of a literary era in the Westcountry, but Jack Clemo leaves a rich legacy. Cornwall and Dorset – and of course Ruth Clemo – are all rightly proud of him.

Rightly or wrongly I have long thought of cricket as a kind of creativity. A cricketing hero of mine, Gilbert Laird Jessop, spent the last twenty years of his life in Dorset. Jessop, who played for Gloucestershire, Cambridge University and England, was one of the biggest hitters in the history of the game.

I never saw him play but in the eye of imagination like to think I did. Wallace Nichols, the poet, saw him unleash his epic innings at the Oval in 1902, and, sitting in a chair that once belonged to

JACK CLEMO, a distinguished Cornishman and writer, who lived his last years with his wife Ruth in Weymouth,where his creativity positively flowed. ▶

Shelley, described it: 'He batted with controlled ferocity,' Wallace told me, 'and he made that very big Oval ground look suddenly small.' They called it 'Jessop's match.' England, batting last, needed 263 to beat Australia on a pitch that was helping the bowlers. When Jessop went in to bat, half the England side was out for just 48 and the match seemingly lost. 'In spirit he was like a Greek god,' said the poet. 'I have never seen the ball hit so hard or so high.' Wallace was recalling an innings he had seen some sixty summers before but he talked as if it were yesterday afternoon. Records show his innings lasted 77 minutes with England winning by just one wicket.

Wallace was a lucky man to have been there and seen that legendary innings, and whenever I go to the county ground at Bristol I picture Jessop crouching at the crease – they called him 'The Croucher' and he didn't like it. Some called him a slogger and he didn't like that either. Moreover it simply wasn't true. He was a wonderful timer of the ball and rarely wasted a scoring opportunity. Mentally, he was looking to score off every ball. Seven times in first class cricket he scored a century in 55 minutes – or less.

Unlike many of the big hitters Gilbert Jessop was equally keen to attack the quick bowlers, relying on footwork and sharp reflexes: a unique and surely a creative cricketer.

Before leaving the cricket scene I must mention a discovery made in 1993: my first visit to Canford School for the second day's play of Dorset v Cornwall in the Minor Counties championship. This surely must be one of the most beautiful grounds in all England. Cricket is a lovely game and when it's played in lovely surroundings there is a deeper magic. Canford has such a magic. A A Milne in a cricketing poem wrote of 'one of those glorious deep blue days …' and that Monday was such a day. Moreover there was the bonus of having lunch with Derek Bridge whom I had seen years ago as captain of Dorset. We talked of these earlier summers, touched on his distinguished Rugby career, and looked ahead to the future and the need for positive purposeful leadership on the cricket field. Derek is now President of Dorset County Cricket Club, and the club is lucky to have such a splendid sportsman at the top.

The past is mysterious.

I believe the reason for the fascination of the past is that by its very nature most of it is lost – lost beyond recall.

In my first-ever meeting with the writer Ronald Duncan sitting in his farmhouse kitchen high on the North Cornwall-North Devon border he asked a question and answered it. 'If a man lives twenty-five thousand days or so, how many of them can he remember? Not more than a couple of hundred at the most. But the rest were days he lived ... they fell like leaves trodden underfoot ...'

And perhaps the same is true of history. Certainly in Dorset there is a strong sense of the past – and mystery. If we go to Badbury Rings, we begin to wonder if this were the site of Arthur's battle of Mons Badonicus. At Badbury Rings we begin to wonder about the character of the Once and Future King. Did he reign in reality or in imagination? We do know that around 410 AD, the Romans were pulling out of Britain to go to the rescue of their disintegrating Roman Empire. The Saxons, a Germanic race, looked towards these islands and then proceeded to colonise by means of the sword. Some say it was Arthur who stemmed the Saxon advance in the south west, and if the Britons had remained united behind Arthur, it is probable the Saxons would have been pushed back into the sea. Bradbury Rings stir our imagination, fan our curiosity.

Or we can go to the Dorset coast and speculate about the smugglers. Writers, especially imaginative storytellers, have usually portrayed our smugglers in romantic fashion; sometimes as young gentlemen more interested in adventure than illicit cargoes and sometimes as double agents in the conflicts between the British and the French. In truth many of the smugglers were capable of violence and murder, treachery and corruption staining their deeds at night.

Out on ancient Dorset locations like Maiden Castle and Knowlton you begin to wonder about the nature of time itself.

The great J B Priestley believed there are three forms of time:

◀ *THREE keen spectators – somebody said 'three wise men' – watching Dorset play Cornwall at cricket on the lovely Canford School ground in 1963. They are – left to right – Canon Ken Rogers, the Cornwall secretary, Derek Bridge, former captain of Dorset County Cricket Club and now President of the county club, and Michael Williams.*

'ordinary time' when I stand on the platform at Bournemouth waiting for a train; 'inner time' when I am quietly contemplating, moments of inner serenity; and 'creative time' when a writer or a painter or sculptor occasionally experiences a phase of 'great intensity.' Mr Priestley, looking back, considers he wrote four complex plays at top speed – in his own words 'like a man watching himself run at headlong pace across a minefield.'

More than once on an ancient landscape I have felt right at the edge of the unknown. On a visit to Maiden Castle I felt '... just one more thing to happen and then *breakthrough*.' Maiden is something of an enigma too: immense and open, yet retaining a secret quality, an energising quality too.

Knowlton also retains its secrets *and* a powerful atmosphere. Jacquetta Hawkes, the archaeologist and widow of J B Priestley said: 'There is something peculiar in the air, an influence ...' and in her section on Knowlton in her *Guide to the Prehistoric and Roman Monuments of England and Wales*, published in 1951, she wrote '... perhaps places where men have felt intensely and acted violently never quite rid themselves of the effects ...'

Getting back to King Arthur, some people are convinced Dorset, or parts of it, is or was King Arthur Country. Now there are certain parts of Cornwall strong in Arthurian atmosphere and association, places like Tintagel, Dozmary Pool and other areas of Bodmin Moor and, of course, the same is true in Somerset, locations like Glastonbury and Cadbury, and I find nothing disconcerting that various Westcountry places make various Arthurian claims. There is a veer to the view that Arthur's was a roving command in that he moved from place to place, rather like General Tito fighting in the mountains of Yugoslavia in the Hitler war.

Some years ago I interviewed a psycho-expansion group in the Westcountry – members of which claimed not only to have lived in Arthurian times but to have been Arthurian characters. These were responsible people doing worthwhile jobs, and their responses led me to this conclusion: one day the reality of Arthur will be proved. Now, there is a prospect.

Two members of that group said Arthur is buried in Dorset. If that is true, then there must be a very good chance of the evidence being found here in Dorset. A member of that psycho-expansion group (people who believe in reincarnation) is of the opinion that in the future an artefact belonging to Arthur will be discovered, and before the cynics scoff they should remember the words of Tom Lethbridge: 'What is magic today will be science tomorrow.'

For centuries men and women have been telling Arthurian stories, but they are deeper and more profound than just good tales. Only an immensely powerful theme, only *something* answering to some deep sense – and need – within the character of Britain and the British could have been sustained for so long.

On any Arthurian journey, we soon discover Arthur is essentially about a search – our search – and secondly at the very heart of the whole process is the quest for our best self – or selves.

Arthur's impact has been so strong, so dramatic that for a long time after his death there was a widely held view he had not died. Some even maintained he would, one day, reappear and drive out the foes – and some of us today feel something of that response beats in many hearts and minds today.

I well remember the morning in 1988 when I read Polly Lloyd's manuscript of *Legends of Dorset*. From her earliest pages Polly showed how the folklore of Dorset has become part of the landscape, and when I finished her last page there was the compulsion to shape a certain question: 'Can there be such a thing as pure legend?' Two questions in fact: 'Can there be smoke without fire?'

I have a hunch – and it is an educated hunch – that legend is often old, very old gossip. Fellow Bossiney author Sally Jones once told me, over a glass of wine, sitting in our garden in North Cornwall, that she thought 'Legends are like a game of "Chinese Whispers" played long ago.' Undoubtedly tales have been passed on, down the generations, through the calendars, and in that process there have been additions and distortions. Apart from the extra dimensions gained in the telling and retelling, the events themselves in some curious way continue to generate an energy of their own.

In her thoughtful introduction to *Legends of Dorset* Polly Lloyd touched on the creative spirit of the place: 'It is a county that has inspired many authors. Jane Austen was particularly fond of Lyme Regis, making the Cobb as famous for being the place where Louisa Musgrove fell in *Persuasion* as it is for being the landing

THE COASTLINE was at the heart of Dorset's secret smuggling past.

point for the Duke of Monmouth at the start of his ill-fated rebellion. John Fowles also chose Lyme Regis as the setting for his modern classic *The French Lieutenant's Woman*. And, of course, Thomas Hardy, arguably Dorset's most famous son, wrote wonderfully evocative accounts of life here.

'But apart from these great works of fiction, Dorset is a treasure house of stories, happy and sad, funny and macabre. Time has occasionally blurred the edges between fact and fantasy, and some of the tales are hard to prove – but just as hard to disprove. Some are as old as time while one or two happened within living memory. But all of them add to the richness of history, these legends of Dorset.'

As someone who has been ghost hunting for more than thirty years, I have a special interest in Dorset's 'other population', but I will basically leave that eerie matter to Peter Underwood, the man acknowledged as Britain's number one ghost hunter. Peter and I have often discussed the nature of ghosts and at this point it might be worth recalling something the poet Robert Graves wrote in a feature, back in 1941, entitled 'What I Believe about Ghosts:' 'The commonsense view is, I think, that one should accept ghosts very much as one accepts fire – a more common but equally mysterious phenomenon. What is a fire? It is not an element, not a principle of motion, not a living creature – not even a disease, though a house can catch it from its neighbours. It is an event rather than a thing or a creature. Ghosts, similarly, seem to be events rather than things or creatures …'

There have been events here in Dorset which positively encourage speculation.

The novelist Muriel Spark once spoke of 'the invisible third ear' an ability to pick up things below the surface of our twentieth century. Maybe some psychic characters have 'a third eye' whereby they are able to see other things. They trust their sixth sense as well as the other five, and have the ability to pinpoint phenomena.

My great hope for the twenty-first century is that it will produce a significant breakthrough for the paranormal. That breakthrough may come in one spectacular leap or a steady accumulation of evidence – or may be a combination of both. In the last fifty years we have seen an incredible building-up of evidence: film and photographs, take recordings and first-hand accounts of events which defy all logical explanation.

But we do look for one major breakthrough and until that moment comes the ghosts of Dorset retain their secrets. For the present they are secret characters and therefore part of *Secret Dorset.*

About the Author

PETER UNDERWOOD, Life President of the Ghost Club Society, is the man rated Britain's number one ghost hunter and has probably heard more firsthand ghost stories than anybody else in the world.

A long-standing member of The Society for Psychical Research, Vice-President of the Unitarian Society for Psychical Studies, a member of The Folklore Society, The Dracula Society and a former member of the Research Committee of the Psychic Research Organisation, he has lectured, written and broadcast extensively. In 1987 he was elected a Fellow of the Royal Society of Arts.

He took part in the first official investigation into a haunting: has sat with physical and mental mediums, and conducted investigations at seances, been present at exorcisms, experiments at dowsing, precognition, clairvoyance, hypnotism, regression; conducted world-wide tests in telepathy and extra-sensory perception, and has personally investigated scores of haunted houses.

Peter Underwood has contributed as many as nine titles to the Bossiney list, his **Ghosts of Cornwall** *and* **Ghosts of Devon** *remain among the Bossiney bestsellers – and his* **Ghostly Encounters** *has just been reprinted. Here he recalls some Dorset hauntings.*

SOMEWHERE IN SECRET DORSET

by Peter Underwood FRSA

SOMEWHERE in secret Dorset you may encounter sea-maidens! A naval commander, anchored in Lulworth, was in his cabin when he was suddenly disturbed by a wild crescendo of shouting and laughing. He raced up the companion ladder, suddenly finding himself, full of fear, in the shadows of the night ... he checked everywhere, seeking to pierce the darkness that was still full of the wild shouts and screams that seemed to be all about him.

Suddenly and inexplicably all the sound stopped, as abruptly as it had begun, and the commander found himself peering into the now silent blackness towards the moonlit foreshore, less than two hundred yards away.

As he watched he saw an evanescent form on the foreshore which he distinguished as a figure of a child, a young girl. He said afterwards that he saw the white-faced girl jerk awkwardly in a macabre dance – and then the girl was joined by another similar figure, and then another and another. He saw the foreshore peopled with a dozen or more girlish wraiths prancing and leaping in a spectacle that was at the same time melancholy and seemingly joyful. It was a strange scene he has never forgotten.

Suddenly the figures stopped dancing, as if obeying an unheard command; the sounds that had returned to accompany the prancing figures, grew faint and as he watched the figures grew fainter and fainter until they disappeared from his view. He peered into the night but the foreshore was now quiet and deserted.

The Lulworth Cove area seems to be conducive to psychic activity. A couple of years ago a correspondent informed me that he and a friend had seen a couple dressed in heavy Victorian clothes on

SUPERSTITION and folklore featured strongly in the life of old Dorset. Here is an ancient photograph of a wishing well.

the beach. They looked so out of place in the bright sunshine and laughing families in bathing costumes but they seemed quite unconcerned and deep in conversation with one another.

My informant told me that he and his companion passed within a couple of yards of the odd couple and almost touched them as they passed. Turning to see whether the eccentric couple were aware of them having passed so close and where the two were heading for, they were astonished to find no sign of the couple! The amazed friends turned and searched everywhere but of the singular couple they had seen so plainly, there was no sign and enquiries about the odd couple from people nearby met with puzzled, vacant gazes. Apparently no one else had seen the Victorian ghosts!

Another correspondent has told me of walking along a road at Lulworth and seeing a shadowy figure that seemed to be following a couple a little way ahead but then it suddenly turned and went through what appeared to be an opening in the high hedge bordering the road.

When my correspondent reached the area she found the hedge completely inpenetrable – in fact there was no opening anywhere along the road. Making enquiries as to anything odd having ever been encountered in the area, she learned that some people had heard a battle re-enactment on a hill nearby, so Lulworth Cove does seem to be a magic, haunted and secret area.

Deep in secret Dorset hide several haunted hotels. In Dorchester the Cornwall Hotel was the billet for numerous American servicemen during the Second World War, many of whom never returned from D-Day. Some of them are thought to be responsible for the many and varied curious happenings that have been reported here ever since.

In particular flames of one sort or another have acted strangely inside the hotel. On more than one occasion normally flickering flames of the log-effect fire in the triangular fireplace in the bar have suddenly shot high for a few minutes before the fire has extinguished itself!

Candles of the splutter-proof variety where the wax does not run stand on a table in the same bar and have behaved in a singular

THE SEA around Lulworth – a magic area.

A DOZEN or more girlish wraiths prancing and leaping …

fashion on occasions, especially it seems when American visitors are in the bar. Once an American was sitting at the table when the candle involuntarily began to splutter and splash and the 'non-running' wax ran down the candle. When the Americans left the bar the candle stopped acting in an unusual manner and resumed burning normally.

Small articles have repeatedly moved without being touched by human hands. Once a single training shoe disappeared for days and was then found elsewhere with the laces twisted and knotted in a pattern not seen before by anyone in the hotel.

The landlord, Steven Evans, has encountered seemingly impossible happenings in the cellar and elsewhere in this comfortable hostelry, happenings that have caused the landlord to vacate that particular part of the premises without delay!

During redecoration in 1994 alarming scratch marks were discovered high up on one wall, as though made by two pairs of claws but the height from floor level ruled out any possibility of the marks being made by the Cornwall's bull terrier.

A local writer has described having a meal at the hotel and while enjoying a chat over coffee afterwards saw the flame of the candle standing on the table suddenly grow taller when the word 'ghost' was mentioned! They moved the candle further away from them on the table in case they were somehow causing the peculiarity but the same thing happened when they said it must be the ghost! Then they tried a little experiment: using words like 'toast' and 'host' and 'boast' they sought to obtain the same result but nothing happened – yet when the word 'ghost' was used once more, the flames immediately grew taller yet again. Finally they decided on something like a test and addressing the affected candle they asked the flame to get smaller if a ghost was responsible and larger if there was no ghost present: the candle flame dramatically reduced itself in size!

Other unexplained happenings occur at the Cornwall Hotel and rightly or wrongly some of those long-dead American servicemen, so fond of practical joking, are usually considered to be responsible. At all events the harmless ghostly activity is now generally accepted and in such a convivial atmosphere perhaps it is not surprising that it continues and thrives.

There is a Dorset secret in Mill Lane, Wimborne, beside the picturesque River Allen, where once stood an 18th century mill. Today the patrons of a comfortable coffee lounge are largely unaware that where they sit a far-reaching drama was once acted out.

In those long-forgotten days a lusty miller became obsessed by a pretty young teenage girl who worked for him and one day, his lust becoming the better of him, he trapped her and forced himself on the weeping child, whose name has come down the years as Annie. Escaping from him at last she fled, distraught, bewildered, betrayed and hurt, hardly knowing where she was going. In her haste to get away she fell into the millstream, striking her head, and she drowned.

Over the years the ghostly form of a wide-eyed teenage girl, in the working-day apparel of two centuries ago, has been seen in and around the area of her suffering, her distress and her death. As recently as the summer of 1994 she was seen on no less than three occasions by three different individuals.

There was the delivery man who told a member of the present staff that they should not let the young lady in fancy dress dart about the premises, he had almost run her down; there was a visitor who asked about the 'pretty young girl' in such picturesque costume she had seen on the way in; and there was a previous owner of Riverside Mews who had twice glimpsed the apparitional girl, once in 1992 and once in 1994, when she was seen in the kitchen area – perhaps the site of her ordeal.

Other reported disturbances include the unexplained ringing of the small table handbells in the restaurant; the falling and smashing of a number of plates (in the presence of several people); the sound of a girl's name – Annie – being called; and the occasional movement of objects: especially remembered is the time when an old-fashioned doll which normally stood on the restaurant sideboard took flight when the son of the owner was passing and it landed on the floor directly in front of him.

Dogs have become agitated in the vicinity of one particular door and, as so often happens in houses reputedly haunted by an individual ghost, electric plugs have been found removed from their sockets, lights have been switched on and off and electrical apparatus has been interfered with. A French girl, a little older than

Annie is said to have been at the time of her death, but perhaps someone whom Annie would find sympathetic, found being alone in the restaurant distressful and she didn't stay long but the regular staff at the time of writing, although often aware that 'Annie' is present, don't really mind the antics and occasional appearance of poor Annie.

Somewhere in secret Dorset you may encounter some of the earliest of oldest ghosts in this country. There are one or two reported Stone Age apparitions (including one on Cranborne Chase) and then there are a few ghostly Roman soldiers at York, at Mersea Island and at Dorset's Corfe Mullen.

Those at Corfe Mullen have been seen in the area of the aptly-named Roman Heights estate. During the whole of the summer of 1993 ghostly Roman soldiers were reported to terrify residents, either by appearing suddenly in the path of a witness and then as suddenly disappearing; by sounds of soldiers marching, the clink of armour and ornaments and the sound of mens' voices speaking in a foreign tongue; or by appearances of Roman soldiers momentarily inside various properties on the estate.

Corfe Mullen was the site of a Roman fortress dating back to AD 45 and a local expert said at the time: 'Yes, there are Roman ghosts in Corfe Mullen. There have been for years. If you live on an ancient site you tend to get emanations from the past. Some people have seen Roman centurions walking through their houses. It's not to be unexpected when the area abounds with Roman burial mounds and a Roman road runs through the estate.'

The ghostly goings on continued for some months and although all is not yet quiet, reliable reports are now few and far between concerning Roman ghosts at Corfe Mullen.

Somewhere in secret Dorset there is a ghost smell. In a cottage nearby three centuries old between Shaftesbury and Sturminster Newton an unexplained smell has been experienced by the present occupants as long as they have been there – more than 25 years.

The origin could never be discovered and eventually they wondered whether it could reveal a 'presence' although they have never seen anything or indeed felt uneasy when the smell is there.

They have noticed that it never comes down the stairs or goes into the main bedroom (both added years after the cottage was built), rather it stays on the landing and occasionally travels into the two adjoining bedrooms.

Discussing the matter with the family it is evident that they have put together quite a list of unexplained happenings, especially noises: the sound of footsteps, a bumping sound and a distinct knock on the bedroom door at the top of the landing; sometimes one bedroom door opening by itself.

From time to time friends and those interested in such matters have watched and waited, hoping to experience the smell; the whole party moving upstairs and waiting, but to no avail. Then another time one of the occupants will go upstairs for something, come down and a short time afterwards go upstairs again and there the smell will be, strong and unmistakable, sometimes so strong as to be almost unbearable but it soon goes; another time it is very faint and will move from one end of the landing to the other end.

In response to the occupants, who wrote to me in the summer of 1994, I said that the sensation of strange smells and paranormal odours in haunted houses have long been reported, along with sounds, visual forms and touchings; and I suggested that it might be an idea to keep a careful record of exactly when the smell is noticed and this may reveal some sort of pattern: perhaps it occurs at times when the human occupants are in a particular mood, be it happy or unhappy or expectant or anxious or whatever; possibly the prevailing weather affects the smell or some other component may become apparent. Certainly the history of the house may play a part in discovering what or who is responsible and I am looking forward to hearing more news of these secret ghostly happenings one day.

Somewhere in secret Dorset you may encounter a werewolf! After a BBC interview at Broadcasting House an employee buttonholed me and told me a curious story: for he had once almost encountered a werewolf.

As a responsible business man he met a lady who was in great trouble and asked him whether he would help her. Her niece had recently come to this country and was staying at her home in Dorset. This young and attractive girl had asked her aunt to do something for her. She said it was very important. Her aunt agreed and the girl asked her to lock her in her room that night and not to let her out or to come into the room until the morning, no matter

THE ghostly form of Annie . . .

what she might hear.

The aunt agreed to help the girl, who was obviously very agitated, and concerned and anxious for what seemed a curious but harmless request. At around two o'clock in the morning the aunt was awakened by the most fearful sounds – including heavy clawing noises and deep sonorous breathing coming from the adjoining bedroom occupied by her niece.

The noises went on and on and she toyed with the idea of going to see what was happening ... she looked at the bedroom door key beside her bed, but she had given her word and she decided to stick to it.

Gradually as dawn broke the fearful sound grew fainter and finally ceased and at last my informant's friend got a little sleep. When she eventually awakened she quickly went to her niece's room where she found the wallpaper stripped from the wall in great stripes and slashes, and everything in the room virtually ripped to pieces, even the mattress and bedclothes had long vicious rips in them. The niece, completely exhausted, lay unconscious on the floor, hunched in an all-fours position like a wolf. Later she said that she had been involved in native rites and practices before she came to England and had been told that while she was away she would turn into a wolf on nights of the full moon.

My informant talked to his friend about the power of suggestion, of psychosomatic disorders, of the power of hypnotism, and he suggested she should persuade her niece to see a psychiatrist. He never heard any more but during his next visit to the West Country he went out of his way to call at the house of the woman who had asked for his help. She was alone and showed him some of the damage wrought in the bedroom used by her niece during her visit; the girl herself had left soon after that awful night saying she was returning to her home in Africa but her aunt wanted nothing more to do with the affair and had severed links with her relatives out there. Now during his visits to West Country friends my informant tells me he deliberately avoids that part of Dorset where, maybe, a werewolf still walks.

In an area of countryside unlike that of any other in Dorset stands Edmondsham House, which has been in the same family for over four centuries, set in quiet landscape between the thick

CUT into the turf of the Downs behind the town of Weymouth is one of England's celebrated White Horses, ridden by George the Third. Maybe this vivid feature of the landscape is no secret, but it gives us a flavour of the mystery and the magic of the past.

woods of Cranborne Chase to the north and the pines of West Moors to the south.

There are records of the manor passing through various hands earlier than 1066 until it was bought in 1563 by Thomas Hussey and he seems to have been responsible for the main core of the present house. Over the years the house has passed through the male and female lines until 1961 the last of four generations of Monro – every one of them called Hector – handed over the manor to his sister's son, Anthony Medlycott, bringing Edmondsham with its ghost story into the same family as Dorset's reputedly most haunted house, Sandford Orcas.

Today Anthony's son, Sir Mervyn Medlycott, has inherited both Sandford Orcas and the baronetcy from his uncle, Anthony's elder brother, while Edmonsham has passed again into the female line and it was recently occupied by Anthony's daughter, Mrs Julia Smith.

The female ghost here was usually seen on the terrace to the west of the house. When some building alterations were being carried out in the East Wing a small and hollow buttress was accidentally knocked down and a skeleton was discovered inside. After the skeleton was buried in consecrated ground for a while the ghost of the mysterious young woman was not seen but during the last couple of years I have received reports of different people on different occasions encountering a beautiful young woman in the west part of the house, a figure that appears to be real and solid and dressed in the costume of a bygone age but in fact a spectral form that disappears when approached too closely.

Somewhere – and perhaps anywhere – in secret Dorset you may witness a UFO. A few years ago a UFO was witnessed at close quarters on Moigne Downs one October night. It was encountered by a family of four who told me they had noticed a fast-moving bright light as they were on their way home late in the evening. The light seemed to focus in on them and almost before they knew what was happening they found themselves in the centre of an enormous spotlight.

They then saw that the light seemed to originate from a completely silent saucer-shaped machine that hovered a short distance from them; the bright light shining from the machine making it difficult to distinguish details but after a couple of moments, moments when they felt they were being subjected to probing examination, the light suddenly shifted and without a sound the enormous saucer-shaped object sped away with incredible speed and was quickly lost to sight. There was no tangible evidence of their encounter but all four witnesses told identical stories when interviewed separately and it is certainly something they have never forgotten.

Oddly enough, on an earlier October night, October 24 1967, two police patrol officers pursued a large illuminated object for twelve miles in the same area. The same UFO, if that is what it was, was reportedly witnessed in other parts of the county at different times that night.

Two days later a former RAF officer was walking his dog one morning across Moigne Downs when, at 11.25am, he noticed something in the sky coming towards him, very fast. When it was

THEY found themselves in the centre of an enormous spotlight . . .

almost directly above him it suddenly almost stopped, hovering silently about 250 feet above the ground. It appeared to consist of a central disc, perhaps 25 feet in diameter and some 12 feet thick. He saw a thick girder-like 'leg' pointing forward towards him and three other 'legs' behind pointing groundwards.

Coming to a complete halt the mysterious object which seemed to have no windows slowly rotated clockwise and then hung there, silent and menacing, for some minutes, the observer continually being pawed by his agitated dog. Finally the front and real 'legs' swung into line close to the main body and the UFO flew off at considerable speed. And in December 1993 Rod Dickinson photographed an 'unknown aerial phenomenon' over Gould's Hill at 11 o'clock in the morning.

Suicide not infrequently gives rise to hauntings, it would seem, and Dorset is no exception in this respect. At Boscombe Manor, once known as Shelley Park since it was the home of Sir Percy Shelley, the poet's son, the library is the most likely place to encounter the ghost of a sad little nursemaid. Once employed in the Shelley household she one day jumped from an upstairs window after a tragic love affair and her ghost haunted the place for years – and perhaps still does.

At the Griffin Hotel at Wimborne the shade of a woman wearing lace-up shoes, a brown skirt and with greying hair is thought to be the unhappy ghost of a mother whose daughter's death drove her to sadness and suicide: her ghost has most frequently been reported at Christmas time, presumably the time of the tragedy.

The well-known Grey Lady of Longham who haunts several private gardens in daylight, drifting almost cloudlike, is thought to be the ghost of a young suicide who destroyed herself at Longham Bridge; while the ghost of a girl who threw herself from the cliffs at Southbourne to her death on the sands below has been seen re-enacting the tragedy accompanied by an eerie scream.

At Branksome Chine the ghostly form of a young ATS suicide has been seen gliding along the beach and reports have persisted ever since the event at the end of 1944. A suicide haunts the upper storeys of Poole's Guildhall; Squire Light of Baglake House, Little Cheney, drowned himself and his ghost haunted the area for many years; and several river banks are occasionally haunted by the ghosts of those whose lives ended thereabouts.

Suicides are unsettled in life and, it would seem, in death also, for they walk in daylight and at night in the areas they knew and loved in happier days. Perhaps some psychic memory lingers after the death of the physical body in parts of secret Dorset.

CASTLES hold their own mystery – this is Corfe Castle depicted on an old postcard.

About the Author

ALISON WEEKS is a Bristolian with her heart firmly rooted in the Westcountry. Educated at Wycliffe School for Girls, Clevedon, she is a well-known Westcountry journalist.

A Scorpio subject, she is interested in history, archaeology – and tap-dancing. Her earlier contributions to the Bossiney list include a chapter entitled 'Harvest of Mystery' in **Wiltshire Mysteries**, *and as co-author she wrote* **Unknown Dorset**. *Now Alison investigates some secrets relating to Dorset's churches.*

'As a child Dorset was synonymous with summer', she says. 'There was so much family history there and the Days Out when we headed for Weymouth, Burton Bradstock or Lulworth were always special. I don't ever remember it raining at all. In fact it was at Weymouth that my parents joined a post-war queue to buy a wedding ring which my father later produced with a flourish on the beach. Sadly the magic moment of proposal was marred by two beastly little boys who popped up from behind a rock smirking.'

DORSET CHURCHES

by Alison Weeks

ALL churches have their secrets – built up through a procession of births, marriages and deaths. Read headstones in a churchyard and there, carved in stone, are snippets of information about the people who lived and died in the parish. Some were laid to rest after exemplary lives. Some died tragically, cut down through illness, childbirth or even violence.

There are the names of tiny children who were powerless to resist the diseases that coursed through communities sweeping away the weak and the strong. But one thing is sure a church is about people. The focal point of life at one time, that building has seen most of life.

Wrapped in the stones of Dorset's ancient churches are the memories and secrets of the people who all played a part in their fabric. Whether famous, philanthropic or just plain, ordinary citizens, each one had a story to tell. And some can still tell theirs.

Search out the tales tucked away in those churches, folded into the hills of Dorset's maternal, enveloping embrace, and joy, despair, hope and good deeds are there.

Dorset has been fought over, conquered by Romans, tamed by the great British king Alfred and suffered at the hands of Cromwell's Parliamentary troops. And the layers of history, from prehistoric weapons and scraps of pottery to the bullet marks of the Roundheads are still around – some of it hidden but much of it still to be seen – if you know where to look.

The fifteenth century St Peter's Church, with its 90-ft high tower, right in the middle of Dorchester, is a splendid medieval building. There is a finely decorated Norman doorway, a fourteenth century Easter sepulchre and a wagon roof which soars above the nave.

But what about the people who have left their stories behind? A magnificent memorial in the north aisle, which at present has been declared in a dangerous state because the mighty piece of carved stonework is parting company with its supporting wall, has a real tale to tell.

Denzil Holles, dressed in stone as a Roman senator in a seventeenth century wig, was undoubtedly a character and something of a diplomat. He was a member of Parliament for Dorchester before the Civil War but managed to survive being accused by King Charles I of high treason and then siding with Parliament, to be finally raised to the peerage after the restoration of the monarchy. Dorchester had sided with Parliament when the civil war broke out in 1642, and although later that year Royalist forces moved into town ransacking the home of St Peter's rector, the parliamentarians managed to hang on to the town. Even Cromwell visited Dorchester in 1645.

MANY of Dorset's lovely old churches retain deep secrets and remain essential characters of ***Secret Dorset****.*

MP Denzil Holles, one of parliament's main leaders and man of fiery eloquence, was definitely not keen on the way the king was managing the country's affairs.

On January 4, 1642 Denzil Holles, John Pym, John Hampden, Arthur Heselrige and William Strode, all members of Parliament, were accused of high treason. The king felt so strongly about this he personally went to the House to arrest them. But word had reached the wanted men earlier in the day and they had taken refuge in the city. And events rapidly followed which plunged England into the bloody battle which set brother against brother and was to tear the county apart for years.

Fighting for the Parliamentary cause, Denzil Holles, a staunch Presbyterian, even raised his own private army – the redcoats. These raw, untrained, largely undisciplined, young men ploughed through the English countryside in company with other Roundhead soldiers, pillaging, thieving and terrorising. But bit by bit a measure of discipline was introduced. Holles' Redcoats fought bravely in many a battle.

Through skill, diplomacy or just sheer cunning, Mr Holles survived his battle with royalty. When the monarchy was restored Denzil Holles was created a baron. Of course it was very much a deliberate act of conciliation on the part of the newly-crowned Charles II. In a bid to disarm criticism not only was Denzil Holles elevated to the peerage and the king's inner council but so were his fellow campaigners Pym and Hampden.

Dorchester obviously thought such an astute man was worthy of tribute and, twenty years after his death, the townspeople put up the magnificent memorial to their famous son.

The Civil War left its marks on other Dorset churches. For what appears such a calm, rural county, it is difficult to imagine Cromwell's troops scouring through the countryside and attacking Royalist strongholds. But they did.

Corfe Castle had seen violence before. The body of young King Edward, who was so brutally murdered by his stepmother Queen Elfrida's henchmen, had been hidden at the castle in 978. And it

◀ *DENZIL Holles remembered in Dorchester.*

was to the martyred young king that Corfe Castle's church was dedicated. The thirteenth century church, close to the spot where the king was murdered, remained almost unaltered for centuries until the Civil War.

Then the peaceful, greystone charm of Corfe was shattered. Into the village marched the Roundheads. The dramatic castle, perched high above the village, was held by Lady Bankes and a pitifully small garrison of retainers and servants. In the absence of her husband Lady Bankes held out against the Parliamentarian forces who were camped below.

Not content with taking shots at the castle and plotting ways of breaking through the fortress's mighty walls, the soldiers set up headquarters in the church. Off came the lead from the roof and windows to make musket balls and down came the organ pipes to hold powder and shot. Prayer books and parish registers were destroyed. Even the rector's surplice was cut up for soldiers' shirts. The magnificent font provided a drinking trough for horses stabled in the church. And a cannon was mounted on the tower, trained on the castle.

Looking at the church nowadays it is difficult to imagine anything other than the reverent stillness that seeps through the ancient building. The Church of St Edward keeps the secret of its rape, quietly out of sight.

It is impossible to watch so many centuries and not see the ebb and flow of life's passions after all. Among church documents are fascinating glimpses into past life in the village of Corfe. One of these is contained in the parish records. After the monarchy was restored Charles II came up with an act to boost the flagging woollen industry – all people had to be buried in woollen shrouds.

But although Corfe's church had suffered so much at the hands of Parliamentarian soldiers it still held on to its dignity. A dignity not granted to many churches. In a glass case in the Baptistry are impressions of the Seals of the Constables of Corfe Castle and Corfe Castle Royal Peculiar Court.

This court, which gave the Rector and choir the right to wear scarlet cassocks, possessed the authority to try matters relating to church law. And rectors were appointed directly by the Crown rather than by the bishop. Sadly Corfe lost this right – along with

FLEET church.

its mayoral privileges and the power to return Members of Parliament – in the nineteenth century.

Flood, fire and tempest all have played a part in some of Dorset's churches. And perhaps nowhere has tempest played a greater part than at the tiny, old church of Fleet, perched on a hill above the 10-mile long Fleet lagoon behind the golden-pebble Chesil Bank.

Fleet, a tiny hamlet close to Weymouth, has seen its fair share of drama. But on November 23, 1924, its ancient pale golden stones were unable to resist the sea which swept up over the Chesil Bank and on up the hill devouring everything in its path. The nave of the church was swept away and so was a cottage close by. Parish clerk of Fleet George Bowering recalled his father James talking of what he had seen as a boy of eleven.

'The sea began to break over the beach at 5am, the water came up as fast as a horse could gallop,' said George. 'James watched as long as he dared, and then, terrified, ran for his life.'

Two old women were rescued from the bedroom window of their house, two other cottages were washed away and a total of seven

THE simple, but beautiful, interior of Fleet Church.

large fishing boats ended up well inland after the sea subsided.

With the church badly damaged and many of the houses lost the rector, George Gould, vowed to build a new village for the parishioners. That church, about a quarter of a mile up the road, is still used today. But the old one, still open to view, crouches in its lush churchyard, ever peering down the valley to watch the mood of the blue grey sheet of water.

People are still very much a part of Puddletown's St Mary's Church. But in this church, with part of the twelfth century tower still in position and the bulk of the building dating back from about 1400, its memories and memorials have been placed there by passing generations.

And Puddletown villagers still burnish the church with life. There is a smell of wood polish and a feeling of well-used holiness. Uneven flagstones worn into shining dips and hollows lead past the fine box pews. And children's coloured drawstring bags hang from ancient woodwork while small desks and chairs nudge splendid, crumbling tombs to long-gone squires and VIPs.

It is a church that relishes life and soaks up great helpings of it. And because it has absorbed so many centuries of change St Mary's has tucked away a wealth of secret treasures just waiting to bring them out for the curious visitor. There are the metal brackets on the end of pews for churchwardens' staffs to keep unruly congregations in line. A perilously broken canopy above a finely carved tomb contrasts with hefty cast iron radiators.

There is a splendid selection of light fittings and even, tucked away on the gallery staircase a bracket for a torch of candle sconce. Canvas fire buckets supplied by the Sun Insurance Company of Bath hang at the back of the church below a musicians' gallery which surely inspired Thomas Hardy to write about the Puddletown choir in his novel *Far from the Madding Crowd.* This church is one of the most perfect examples of the work of William Laud who, as Archbishop of Canterbury, systematically worked through churches under his jurisdiction.

The archbishop was a man of energy and wanted to see the Church sorted out and that meant repairing, restoring and improving parish churches including Puddletown's. The vicar and parishioners of Puddletown were asked what was needed at their church. One of the main pillars was crumbling, the seats were no good and more space was needed for worshippers, they told him. The result of their request – which cost £130 – can still be seen today.

But once more, even at Puddletown, the hand of the Civil War was at work. The church interior is undoubtedly a fine tribute to that man's vision. But what went on behind the scenes was yet another step towards the end for Charles I.

William Laud had earned the king's respect. They shared the same vision of an efficiently organised church and Laud embarked on his massive tidying-up exercise. But this did not go down so well with the people. The son of a Reading tradesman, Laud, a small red-faced man, lacked the social graces. Many of his colleagues on the King's council though him difficult and ill-bred.

Ill-bred he may have been but there can be little doubt that the view he and Charles shared of beauty and order has been executed with skill at Puddletown.

The work was started right away in 1635 and that date is shown on the front of the gallery. The restoration took a couple more years and in time the altar with its surrounding rails was installed, the pulpit and prayer desk, the west gallery and the wonderful oak box pews with their brass hinges. According to the late Arthur Helps, vicar of St Mary's earlier this century: 'The interior of the building is especially interesting because we have here, practically unchanged, the village church just as it was three centuries ago.'

And Sir Frederick Treves writing in his book on Dorset says: 'The feature of greatest interest in Puddletown is the church, one of the few in the county which has been happy in escaping the hand of the restorer. No church can compare with this in human interest and nowhere can one come into closer touch with the Dorset of the past.'

A blocked doorway in the south wall of Bere Regis church has a fascinating story. The landowning family, the Turbervilles, who for centuries lived in the parish, were interwoven with the fabric of this church. And legend says that one Turberville fell out with the vicar vowing never to enter the church again. Later when the breach was healed the squire still felt unable to break his vow – so a new doorway was built to that he could attend church once more without breaking his vow.

In fact the Turbervilles, who provided the inspiration for Thomas Hardy's novel Tess of the D'Urbervilles, were patrons of this splendid church for nearly five hundred years. The family became lords of the manor during the 13th century and continued in an unbroken line until the family finally died out in the early 18th century.

Hardy must have known the church at Bere Regis well. In the novel which sees the tragic heroine Tess climb from the pit of poverty only to be cast down again and again, Hardy described the Turberville tombs in the south aisle: *'They were canopied, altar-shaped and plain, their carvings being defaced and broken; their brasses torn from their matrices, the rivet holes remaining like martin-holes in a sand-cliff.'*

Tucked away in a corner of the south aisle is a floor slab paying tribute to a long-gone Turberville. This stone, to John Turberville

STAINED glass and carved wood – a tribute to the craftsmen who restored the church at Puddletown.

A STONE tomb at Puddletown.

and his wife Anne, both of whom died in 1633, has been left in the floor while other slabs were taken up last century when the floors were repaved. This illustrious family seems ever-present in Bere Regis church. Well-worn so that its inscription is barely legible is another slab in the south aisle – the entrance to the Turberville vault.

Age and tradition are folded into the medieval stones of the tiny 45ft long St Martin's Church in Wareham. This splendid little church is reputed to be the resting place for Brictric, king of the West Saxons. And it is said to owe its origin to the first bishop of Sherborne St Aldhelm. There are still fascinating bits of Anglo-Saxon masonry hidden away on St Martin's church which stands just above the road looking more secular than divine. Rather like an ancient, over-tall house the church has fallen in and out of favour over the centuries.

THE CHURCH at Bere Regis. ▶

In 1762 when a massive fire raged through Wareham, St Martin's provided shelter for many families who lost their homes to the blaze. But even then the poor church's popularity had waned and it had been disused since 1736.

St Martin's, which was probably rebuilt about 1020 and refurbished when William the Conqueror took charge of England, lay unused for another two centuries. Apart from a couple of christenings and a commemorative service for Queen Victoria's jubilee in 1887 the little church lay disregarded until 1935. Just why the tiny church has been so unloved over the centuries is a secret which she probably keeps to herself. Fortunately in the 1930s the Archdeacon of Dorset spotted St Martin's and decided to set up a committee to organise its renovation.

That simple restoration work was recorded with a plaque put up in the church porch: '*After two centuries of silent witness this ancient church of St Martin was rededicated to the service of Almighty God by Neville, Lord Bishop of Salisbury, 23rd November 1936.*' Just three years later an effigy of the charismatic campaigner of the Arabian cause T E Lawrence was presented to the little old church by Lawrence's brother. T E Lawrence, who lived at Cloud's Hill Cottage near Bere Regis for some of his life, used often to visit Wareham, and the effigy showed him in full Arab dress grasping the hilt of a curved dagger.

St Martin's Church, which in the mid-1990s was undergoing a further restoration project with services once more suspended, yielded up some of its hidden history during its previous restoration.

Workmen in 1940 were surprised to uncover fragments of wall decorations dating from the twelfth to the eighteenth century. There were traces of painted decoration from an Elizabethan black-letter text to an eighteenth century memorial to Carruther and his wife who died of 'Typhus favour'.

And another curiosity was a door beside the altar which may have been evidence of a Christian superstition that the Devil would flee through it when the bells began to ring.

About the Author

FELICITY YOUNG, who was educated at Lord Digby's Grammar School, Sherborne, has a great affection for Dorset. A water colour painter, she has contributed many illustrations to Bossiney's growing list of Dorset titles, and her written work includes a chapter in **Strange Dorset Stories**. *It concerns Charlotte Bryant, a small-time prostitute.*

Felicity Young, who lives at Tintagel in North Cornwall, has made a special study of King Arthur and related legends and is co-author of **King Arthur in the West**. *She has made radio broadcasts on the Once and Future King and the craft of illustrating books. She is an accomplished horsewoman and teaches Yoga.*

In this, her latest contribution to the Bossiney list she makes three in-depth studies of three well-known personalities in an attempt to find out what made them tick.

THREE LEGENDARY CHARACTERS

by Felicity Young

JUDGE Jeffreys, Lillie Langtry and Lawrence of Arabia – three very different characters, three very different lives. But can they be part of *Secret Dorset*?

The truth is facets of their character – and characters – remain secret. There may have been passion in their lives, but there is an iceberg quality in all three: 'the small visible part of something especially a problem or difficulty …'

All three paid a heavy price for their fame – and maybe as a result of those prices paid emerged with personalities that were either enigmatic or ambiguous – or both.

George Jeffreys, though actually not a Dorset man, being of Welsh descent, played an important role in the shaping of the county's history. He became renowned for his ruthless sentencing but it was his treatment of the rebels who took part in Monmouth's rebellion that really triggered his reputation as the 'Hanging Judge'. He became known as 'Bloody Judge Jeffreys' and was much hated especially in the Westcountry.

Jeffrey's Bloody Assizes sentenced to death men who, largely due to lack of work and money, had been easily recruited by Monmouth as he swept through the West. Lyme, Weymouth, Sherborne, Poole, Bridport and Wareham were all scenes of execution. The Oak Room in Dorchester saw as many as 250 men sentenced to death, pleas of not guilty were futile. Judge Jeffreys was at his cruel peak. After Dorset he travelled into Devon and Somerset; Exeter, Taunton and Bristol were all part of the Bloody Assizes. Out of the 1500 men who stood trial only 79 were pardoned, of the rest some 400 were executed, around 850 sentenced to transportation, the remainder either flogged, fined or imprisoned. The blood-bath finally over Jeffreys returned to London where he was to become the youngest-ever Lord Chancellor, a highly motivated man who had achieved a very important office at the relatively early age of 40.

So what kind of man was he? His reputation is one of a bloodthirsty, ruthless and foul-mouthed man, married twice, with six children; he had followed in his grandfather and father's footsteps with a career in the courts. He had been a good student though he admitted to having a 'Celtic' temperament. He was often deeply depressed and gloomy then at the other extreme loud, forceful and vociferous, probably not the best attributes for a judge but Jeffreys climbed from the lowest rungs of the judicial ladder to the very top of his profession. In court he could be lenient or extremely hard on whoever stood before him in the dock. Before and after the Bloody Assizes he always kept to the letter of the law. It may have seemed bloodthirsty to dish out sentences of hanging, drawing and quartering, a particularly barbaric practice but the seventeenth century was a barbaric age. Women were still burned at the stake and small children pilloried for what seem now to be minor crimes. Jeffreys was only doing what other judges of his day would do. He was fiercely passionate about his religion and defended his king with equal fervour, probably the reason for his merciless treatment of the Dorset rebels. It was patriotism in the extreme. He saw a union between Church and Crown as the foundation for a strong Tory government; any threat to this was cause for harsh punishment. In his eyes they were traitors and the punishment for treason was death.

Jeffreys was unfortunate that he lived in the age of the pamphleteer. The power of the pen was as mighty then as it is today and he was harshly treated by the writers of the day. Jeffreys was subjected to a trial by media instigated by the Whig pamphleteers. He wrote: 'Curse my fortune that I ever should have been born in a time of printing'. I expect there are a number of latter-day judges and politicians who hold the same sentiment. He became a scapegoat for his fellow Tories and finally died in the Tower.

Looking at a painting of this legendary character it is hard to see any evil in his eyes. He appears to be a mild gentle man but history tells us this is not so. He was obviously a man of principles who believed in patriotism but savage and brutal? Perhaps no more so than his contemporaries. To judge him against today's standards of humanity would be wrong and highly unfair; to find out about the real Judge Jeffreys you would need to study seventeenth century history in detail before passing sentence.

If he were guilty of anything, it was of 'Loving the Church and loathing Dissent'. He was an ardent Tory and royalist who did not suffer fools lightly. He had a quick temper but these bouts of temper would often coincide with the recurrence of his kidney stone problem. He had a reputation for drinking but the somewhat theatrical circumstances of the court and Jeffreys's rather loud and flamboyant manner may well have fuelled this assumption. To dub the man as a monster just because his behaviour was arrogant, impetuous and sarcastic would have been playing into the hands of his critics. There are many other cases throughout history where uprisings, plots and rebellions have been dealt with such ferocity, Judge Jeffreys was not alone in his hard line of punishment. This was not a unique act of savagery inflicted on the 'peasants' of the Westcountry but in keeping with the policies of the government of the day. So, to make Jeffreys not only a scapegoat for his own party in his own historical time, but also a scapegoat for the horrors of several centuries of crimes against humanity is convenient. He was definitely not a saint but, on the other hand, he may not have been the devil that propaganda made him out to be.

The legend of Judge Jeffreys continued to grow even after he was dead and buried. Some of his more fortunate 'victims' who had lived to tell the tale crawled out of the woodwork to give their accounts of Jeffreys's treatment of them. Most of these accounts were grossly exaggerated and inaccurate, but all added fuel to the fire. Jeffreys's character assassination went on well into the nineteenth century, the stories growing and changing like Chinese Whispers, until, at the end of it all whom do we believe? History has thrown up some fascinating personalities, some evil some good. It is hard to decide on which side of the line George Jeffreys should be placed.

The public love to hear of a Royal romance, better still a Royal scandal. Today's media goes to town exposing a couple to constant hounding from hopeful photographers and reporters in search of an exclusive, watching for any indiscretion. Human nature makes us curious to know how other people live. We want to know of their fortunes and misfortunes – that is why 'soap' operas are so popular. In Victorian times however such news did not make the headlines. It was confined to the society pages and if there was a hint of scandal, apart from being the highlight at a few ladies' tea parties, it was conveniently buried – certainly it was not the business of the 'man in the street'. Because of the degree of privacy Royalty was then allowed, unlike the Royals of today, they could carry on their lives with a certain amount of freedom.

The Prince of Wales, Bertie, later to become Edward VII, was well known in society for his flirtations but, sheltered from the press, he was able to enjoy his dalliances without the disapproval of the general public. It was the age of the double standard, a time of high moral tone, but affairs were undertaken as if by mutual agreement between husband and wife; acceptable as long as there was no scandal. Divorce was to be avoided at all cost, so it was easier to have an amicable agreement allowing married men and women virtually to do as they pleased.

It was on to this fickle scene that there came a remarkable woman who captured the heart of the Prince of Wales and, it might be said, of every man who laid eyes on her. Lillie Langtry was very beautiful but she had other qualities, too, which made her attractive.

She had been brought up with six brothers which undoubtedly made her rather forthright. Having to stand up for herself gave her an air of confidence which made her stand out from the crowd of society beauties. It was a time when women were judged more for their looks than their character or their intelligence and it made a refreshing change to find a lady with brains and beauty. Not having been born into society, though her father was the Dean of Jersey,

LILLIE Langtry, a royal mistress, the most talked-about young lady of her day. Yet chapters of her life remain secret. Entitled 'A Jersey Lily', painted by John Everett Millais, this was Lillie's favourite portrait of herself.

she had to make her entry into it by different means. She was seen at social functions with her husband Edward Langtry, an Irishman from a respectable family in Belfast, who would not allow her to attend alone but who was obviously bored by the whole scene. It was not long before she was painted and sketched by artists who admired her and was launched on the general public by one particular print which was readily available to buy. Frank Miles was responsible for the original, sketched hurriedly at a party. It was this small drawing that started Lillie out on the road to fame, and she became one of the most admired 'professional beauties' of her day. She later sat for Millais and Edward Poynter but the power of the printing press and the camera were such that she quickly reached a much wider public. She soon caught the attention of Bertie, Prince of Wales, and they began a relationship which was to last ten years. It started as a secret liaison but soon developed into a more public affair.

They could be seen together on many occasions, in fact Bertie made Lillie his first 'public love'. He had never openly flaunted a mistress until then; Lillie was obviously different. Instead of giving her expensive jewels, he built her a house in Bournemouth where they could spend time together. Because of her eagerness to be accepted into society she sat for artists and photographers at every opportunity and her face soon became famous in nearly every household. When she rode out on Rotten Row in a flattering black habit on a horse given to her by an admirer, people began to recognise the 'Jersey Lily', the face from Millais' portrait hung at the Royal Academy and the beauty on the cards available at the corner shop. Bertie and Lillie were the talk of London.

What was it about this woman that drew the Prince so strongly to her? What was her secret attraction that she could beguile men in such a fashion? She was not only admired by gentlemen but many ladies saw much in her character, looks and behaviour that was admirable. She had many close friends, one of whom surprisingly enough was Alexandra, Bertie's wife. There must have been times when she felt out of her depth, especially at the start of her entry into society when she admitted she felt no better than the housemaids, unable to dance, plainly dressed and confused by the cutlery at dinners. But she always kept her sense of purpose and rose from an unknown to a highly accepted member of society in a short space of time.

It was her ambition to be well known and well liked but her relationship with Bertie was probably more than even she could have hoped for. She was a sensuous, passionate woman with an air of confidence about her, that many women would have tried hard to achieve, but to her it came naturally. She loved sailing and her horses and horse-riding, something she had in common with the Prince of Wales, and enjoyed a day at the races. In many ways they were well suited, Bertie was something of a rebel very much like Lillie. He also had great energy, courage and was clearly an interesting, exciting man. Lillie was unhappy with her life and her marriage, and was drawn towards this daring Prince, to begin a long-lasting friendship. Lillie had other liaisons and so did Bertie but the years they spent together were very special. Lillie did not regret her situation, in love with another woman's husband, for one minute. In fact she was philosophical about it and said: 'In life I have had all that I really wanted very much – a yacht, a racing stable, a theatre of my own, lovely gardens'. After her affair with Bertie she went into the theatre and spent some years performing to full houses, she was a very talented and beautiful woman who led a rather public life but underneath was a very private person.

T E Lawrence, better known as Lawrence of Arabia, is part of mysterious Dorset. His later life revolved around the small cottage he owned in the Dorset countryside and a stretch of quiet Dorset road holds the secret of his untimely death.

The cottage, Clouds Hill, was almost derelict, there was very little furniture and no luxuries of any kind. But that was how Lawrence wanted it. He placed little value on material possessions except perhaps for his powerful motorcycle and his cottage, both of which were symbolic. They provided him with a means of escape from the harsh realities of life. He saw Clouds Hill as a refuge to which he could flee when the pressures of public attention threatened. The press were just as persistent in the 1920s as they are today and they hounded Lawrence, the 'war hero' unmercifully, even when, under an assumed name, he joined first the RAF and then the Army and finally returned to the RAF. He no longer wanted his rank of Colonel – he just wanted to be plain private in every sense of the word, finding peace in what he called his 'Swiss Family Robinson' cottage.

T E Lawrence was an enigmatic figure. He seemed to be different things to different people. He was a well-educated man who was interested in archaeology and medieval history. Many of his friends were writers or poets, indicative of his sensitive nature. He had experienced all the horrors and rigours of war and the disillusionment of politics and by the time he came to Dorset he was in need of solitude.

T E LAWRENCE longed to escape from the glare of publicity. When serving as a private at the Royal Tank Corps Camp here in Dorset, he acquired a secluded derelict cottage and restored it. Clouds Hill became his oasis but today it is the focus of unanswered questions relating to Lawrence's strange death.

Clouds Hill was the centre of his world, only a short distance from Bovington Camp where he had been posted as private T E Shaw. People drifted in and out, listening to music on the gramophone, reading poetry and generally meditating on life. The cottage was stark in appearance with a thought-provoking inscription above the front doorway, echoing Lawrence's feeling that there should be nothing within the four walls to tie him down or cause him to worry. It was a very cultural place, visited by many well-known authors and poets. Among them were Siegfried Sassoon, Robert Graves, E M Forster, the Shaws and the Hardys.

These visitors to Clouds Hill were also his close friends and to many of them he wrote prolifically. From his letters his moods could clearly be gauged, he wrote with sadness, humour and sometimes contentment, obviously a very emotional man. Then for some strange reason, one that his friends could not fathom, he sent postcards saying he would not be writing many letters in future. This was shortly before he died.

T E Lawrence wanted nothing more than to be left alone by the pursuing press. He left the army and Clouds Hill to return to the RAF. He was given a far-flung posting in India which should have been sage enough but for an uprising in Afghanistan. The press got wind of his whereabouts and speculated that the presence of Lawrence, the infamous arch-spy must mean some kind of secret mission. It required a daring escapade to by-pass the waiting journalists when he finally returned to England.

Once more in England, but not at his beloved Clouds Hill, he found contentment as a mechanic tinkering with seaplanes at the Flying Boat Station in Plymouth Sound. He proved to be a versatile man, from archaeologist to intelligence officer and from war hero to simple mechanic.

After he left the services he spent more time at Clouds Hill, but its location was known to the press and from time to time they would, much to his great annoyance, lie in wait for him hoping for a photograph. He was well aware that his 'legend' would never let him live in peace. He often told his friends he wanted to be seen as mere mortal not some super-human. The newspapers, always hungry for an exclusive, could not accept that such an exciting and successful personality would want anonymity, to become a nobody.

His only other escape route was to go for a ride on his huge Brough Superior motorcycle. He had owned several over the years and had always transferred the name 'Boanerges' meaning 'Sons of Thunder' to each one. He had a passion for speed and often admitted driving himself and his machine to the limit. He had quite a reputation for his daring exploits.

On his motorcycle, distance and weather conditions were no object, he enjoyed the challenge of the open road. Visiting his friends often took him many miles from home, so it was particularly ironic that his death should occur such a short distance from home and on a clear bright morning.

On Tuesday May 13 1935 he took his motorcycle from Clouds Hill to the camp to send a telegram to his friend Henry Williamson asking him to visit him at the cottage the next day. It should have been a journey like any other, but as he travelled at speed along this stretch of road, one that he had no doubt travelled hundreds of times before, fate took the upperhand.

Apparently there were two errand boys on bicycles cycling along the road from the camp. Lawrence swerved to avoid them but made contact with a wheel of one of the bicycles. He lost control of his motorcycle and in a split second he went over the handlebars and hit the road, losing consciousness immediately. He never regained consciousness in fact, remaining in a coma for six days. He died in the Bovington Camp Hospital on May 19 having never revealed the true circumstances surrounding the accident.

It was inevitable the death of such a man should be shrouded in mystery. He had been the focus of attention as a spy and an activist. There were those who could not accept his death as anything but suspicious and wove tales of conspiracy, murder and, some even suggested, suicide. Could there have been anything more sinister on that Dorset road on that bright, clear May morning in 1935? Or was it simply fate that brought together those two young boys and the reluctant hero?

The sudden death of Lawrence of Arabia was mourned worldwide. But there were many questions left unanswered. Might he have played an important role in the Second World War or would he have shunned the call of the nation and continued to seek solitude in the Dorset countryside? A man with his unquestionable talents would have been a valuable asset to his friend and admirer Winston Churchill. But whether his death was accidental or engineered the world lost an exceptional man.

His funeral took place at Moreton Church, a few fields away from his precious Clouds Hill. His grave is in an annexe, a short distance from the churchyard. A magnificent sculpture mounted on a huge tomb depicting Lawrence the 'crusader' is to be found in St Martin's Church, Wareham. It was originally intended for Salisbury Cathedral but the Dean would not accept it. Their loss was undoubtedly Wareham's gain as it is a beautiful portrayal of Lawrence in full Arab dress, sculpted by Eric Kennington. It seems appropriate that because of Lawrence's connections with Dorset that the tomb should find a resting place within the county.

Lawrence of Arabia lived a very 'secretive' life. He was a secret man, charismatic, much loved and admired by his friends but very much the loner, and the mystery surrounding his death only served to make him more of an enigma.

More Bossiney Books ...

SECRET CORNWALL
Introduced by Madeleine Gould

SECRET DEVON
Introduced by Sarah Foot

GHOSTS OF DORSET
by Peter Underwood
'... an eerie exploration by Britain's number one ghost hunter.'

ABOUT EXMOOR
by Polly Lloyd
'It is a cameo to be treasured,' says Polly Lloyd who takes us on a reflective tour of this timeless corner of England.'
Book Journal

LEGENDS OF DORSET
by Polly Lloyd
The author explores legendary Dorset, visiting places as diverse as the Sacred Circle at Knowlton and Chesil Beach. Dorset is a mine of myth and folklore..
'Weird happenings ...' Polly Lloyd delves through tales ranging from moving rocks to murders.
Frank Kempe, North Devon Journal-Herald

CURIOSITIES OF EXMOOR
by Felicity Young
'... a tour in words and pictures of the National Park embracing Somerset and Devon.'
Nancy Hammonds, Evening Herald
'Felicity Young, an artist who has contributed many drawings to Bossiney Books, makes her debut as an author with a beautiful description of Exmoor and its many delights.'
June Glover, South Hams Group of Newspapers

PSYCHIC PHENOMENA of the WEST
by Michael Williams
The subject of a Daphne Skinnard interview in BBC Radio Cornwall
'Michael Williams continues his well-known researches into the strange and inexplicable ... cases range from Cornwall to Wiltshire ...'
The Cornish Guardian

SUPERSTITION AND FOLKLORE
by Michael Williams. 44 photographs.
A survey of Westcountry Superstitions: interviews on the subject and some Cornish and Devon folklore.
'... the strictures that we all ignore at our peril. To help us to keep out of trouble, Mr Williams has prepared a comprehensive list.'
Frank Kempe, North Devon Journal-Herald

STRANGE STORIES FROM DEVON
by Rosemary Anne Lauder & Michael Williams. 45 photographs.
Strange shapes and places, strange characters, the man they couldn't hang, and a Salcombe mystery, the Lynmouth disaster and a mysterious house are some of the strange stories from Devon.
'... full of good stories, accompanied by many photographs of local happenings which have mystified'
Mary Richards, Tavistock Times